Andrew Williams is an experimental psychologist with 20 years of experience conducting interviews in academic, government and private firms. He was raised in England, where he earned a Bachelor of Science in psychology, and immigrated to the US in the 1980s where he earned his Masters in psychology. Andrew's career is in social science research where he has overseen the administration of interviews to over half a million people, to answer questions such as: How do tax payers want their money spent? Is there a Gulf War syndrome? What happens to adopted children? Do students get the education they deserve? What do employees think of their bosses? What causes people to go bankrupt?

Andrew has written dozens of technical reports, authored journal articles and regularly presents papers at international conferences. He served as a Guest Researcher at the National Institute of Mental Health where he was granted an award by the Foundation for Advanced Education in the Sciences for his research on cocaine.

Andrew's knowledge of psychology also has a very personal element. In 2001, after 17 wonderful years of marriage, Andrew lost his wife and best friend to mental illness. Since that time he has focused on educating others about personality strengths and foibles.

Andrew's expertise and comfortable writing style, enable him to decipher psychological secrets buried in obscure reports and divulge them to readers in a unique and revealing manner. He has examined thousands of research studies and summarised the most interesting to entertain and inform. Andrew lives with his three children and collection of African masks in rural USA.

Contact the author at: info@howdoyoucompare.com

ANDREW N. WILLIAMS

THE TRUTH ABOUT YOU

DISCOVER HIDDEN TRUTHS ABOUT YOURSELF – AND ENHANCE YOUR LIFE

Vermilion
LONDON

1 3 5 7 9 10 8 6 4 2

First published in the USA in 2004 as *How Do You Compare?* by The Berkley Publishing Group

First published in the United Kingdom in 2004 by Vermilion, an imprint of Ebury Press
Random House UK Ltd, Random House, 20 Vauxhall Bridge Road, London SW1V 2SA

Random House Australia (Pty) Limited
20 Alfred Street, Milsons Point, Sydney, New South Wales 2061, Australia

Random House New Zealand Limited
18 Poland Road, Glenfield, Auckland 10, New Zealand

Random House (Pty) Limited
Endulini, 5A Jubilee Road, Parktown 2193, South Africa

Random House UK Limited Reg. No. 954009
www.randomhouse.co.uk
Papers used by Vermilion are natural, recyclable products
made from wood grown in sustainable forests.

A CIP catalogue record is available for this book from the British Library.

ISBN: 0091900131

Designed by seagulls

Printed and bound in Great Britain by Mackays of Chatham plc, Chatham, Kent

This book is written to entertain and educate. It is not a diagnostic tool for those seeking
clinical help. These tests are here to help you learn about yourself, not to elevate you to a
lofty university position, condemn you to a life of servitude or spark a depressive episode.
As a researcher administering these tests, I have a responsibility to help you, not to give you
problems. While it is my hope that this book may help shed light on your personality and
give you insights on others, it is not a replacement for professional counselling.

For my favourite respondents: DW, FAW, EGW and GW.
ANW

This book is dedicated to all of those who have conscientiously taken part in a research study, answered a questionnaire or helped a fellow researcher over the telephone; you are in the pages that follow. Without you, this book would not be possible. Thank you and enjoy.

CONTENTS

Preface   ix
Acknowledgements   xiii

1 INTELLIGENCE   1
Intelligence Test   7

2 CREATIVITY   41
Wordsmith's Creativity Test   49
Engineer's Creativity Test   55

3 RELATIONSHIPS   81
Relationship Satisfaction Test   86
Strength of Relationship Test   93

4 SEX AND DESIRE   125
Test of Sexual Opinions   131
Sexual Experiences and Desires Test   148

5 HAPPINESS 173
Happiness Test 179
Cheerfulness Test 185
Cheerfulness Test for Your Friend 191
The Peak Experiences Test 204

6 MOTIVATION AND CONTROL 229
Locus of Control Test 235

7 PERSONALITY OVERVIEW 261

Epilogue 279
References 281
Index 296

PREFACE

I study people for a living. I give them surveys and tests and analyse the results. I have been responsible for arranging interviews with over half a million individuals, and when people discover what I do for a living, they always ask me to tell them something interesting about themselves. So, like a psychological palm reader, I always keep a few personality facts on hand to impress the inquisitive. For example, did you know that you can increase your IQ by chewing gum, more intelligent women have better sexual fantasies and it is far easier to fall in love after vigorous exercise? Although virtually everybody (either secretly or openly) wants to learn more about themselves, they don't want to answer a lot of stupid questions before they get the answers. I don't blame them – I've seen many poorly designed tests. But I have also found some wonderful, insightful, fun-to-take tests.

Recently, it dawned on me: 'Wouldn't it be terrific if someone who knows about personality tests picked the easiest, most interesting tests and assembled them into a book?' I started to do it, but I couldn't stop there. I have learned that when people take a personality test, they want to learn three things:

1. How they scored on the test.

2. What their answers mean.

3. How did *others* score?

Getting your score is no good unless you can gauge yourself against other test takers. In essence, people want to know *What's the truth about me?* The answer is in your hands.

With this text, you will learn more about yourself than reading a bookstore full of self-improvement books. I have reviewed thousands of psychological studies. Most are filled with psychobabble that is both difficult and tedious to read. However, there are some gems in the heap out there. I have extracted dozens of the most intriguing studies and briefly presented their results for you in a fresh, relaxed style. While writing these comparisons I have pictured you and myself having a comfortable conversation at a party or a restaurant.

The structure of each chapter is simple: learn about an interesting part of your mind, take a quiz to immediately learn more about your personality, then compare yourself to thousands of others who have taken the same test. I have used plenty of examples to make abstract psychological ideas tangible and fun. Be warned, however, that I have taken liberties by extrapolating the findings of some studies. Psychologists, like all good scientists, tend to be conservative when attributing their findings to others. I have taken their results and applied them to the real world. I have also cited every research paper mentioned so you can look up the studies and learn more about them if you wish. I find the social sciences fascinating and exciting. After reading this book, I think you will too. Enjoy.

ANW
October 2004

ACKNOWLEDGEMENTS

This book started off as an idea; I knew the idea would make a good book, but I had not written a book before, so I did what I do best – conducted some research. I found a terrific author of fifteen books to lead me in the right direction and provide technical assistance. Thank you, Dr Boris Allan; without you, this book would not be possible.

I have always worked in the social sciences, and although I love words, I am more familiar with reading esoteric psychology texts rather than literature. Paul K. Hadfield has been tremendous in assisting me translate abstruse technical terms and a plethora of semi-related thoughts into readable English. Thanks, Paul!

Having an idea and writing a book is fine. However, navigating the world of publishing requires a specialist. Madeleine Morel is everything an agent should be. Madeleine's knowledge, diligence and creativity helped transform an idea into this book. My superlative agent brought me to a wonderful editor. Thank you to Random House's Amanda Hemmings and Julia Kellaway for your vision and enthusiasm.

Being a good survey methodologist, I had to pilot test draft copies of this manuscript to volunteer subjects. Feedback and assistance from the following people honed and clarified the final product: Kathie, Debbi, Pete, Dave, Martha, Jean, Jim, Kathleen, Ian, Norman, Forrest, Emily and Grace.

1

INTELLIGENCE

Let me have a little think. ALBERT EINSTEIN

WHAT IS INTELLIGENCE?

While you probably have a pretty good idea of what intelligence is, your description of intelligence may differ from others. This is precisely one of the major problems in psychology. Definitions of *intelligence* include 'the ability to carry on abstract thinking' and 'basic reasoning ability'. There is also a notion that intelligence is like a mood – it can ebb and flow through our daily lives. Whatever you consider intelligence to be, don't be fooled into thinking that intelligence is what intelligence tests measure. The rest of this chapter will dispel that idea.

THE TRUTH ABOUT YOU

Intelligence or IQ?

Before we go further, let's clarify some terminology. To many people the term *IQ* is synonymous with intelligence. This is not quite accurate. IQ stands for *intelligence quotient*. Your IQ is merely a figure that corresponds to the number of correct answers you selected on a test. The *quotient* part is your mental age as measured by a test, divided by your chronological age in years (multiplied by 100). In this chapter, the term *IQ* is preferred when discussing test results. You can decide if IQ tests truly measure intelligence.

A Brief History of Intelligence Testing: How We Got Here

Intelligence testing has a chequered history, a chequered present and, by most accounts, will have a chequered future. In many ways Charles Darwin's *The Origin of Species* is responsible for modern IQ testing. In 1859, Darwin knocked humans off their lone pedestal when he tied us to the apes. The impact of *The Origin of Species* on the scientific community was enormous. By the late 1800s many scientists were desperately trying to distance humans from our simian cousins. Yet it was also thought that comparing the two species would provide answers about which characteristics indicate intelligence.

But as evolution was a new subject, scientists of the day were naïve. They didn't know what characteristics to assess. So they started looking at obvious things to measure. Since apes have long forearms, scientists of the day decided that short forearms must indicate intelligence. So everyone had their arms measured to see how smart they were.

Back in the 1890s a dedicated Italian physician, Cesare Lombroso, thought he could predict who would become a criminal by measuring the gap between the big toe and the other toes. His idea was that since apes have a gap between their toes, criminals (whom he believed were unintelligent) must too. Dr Lombroso, a man of science, dutifully measured the toes of prostitutes, looking for data.

Eventually, psychologists of the late nineteenth century began to apply this theory to brain size. Was the key to measuring intelligence the quantity of grey matter? Several studies compared the brain weights of deceased scientists and professors to those of executed criminals. The problem with this method of research was that subjects had to be dead to be measured. Soon psychologists of the era decided that measuring the skull itself was good enough and the science of 'craniometry' became wildly popular. In the late 1800s, getting your head measured was in vogue. School children, professors, criminals and people from cultures around the globe were brought into labs to have their craniums circumnavigated. It was believed that large heads and high foreheads indicated high intelligence.

Craniometricians were not simply overzealous crackpots. This 'science' was conducted by some of the most renowned researchers of the day. Even the groundbreaking educationist Maria Montessori believed in the cranial capacity arguments. She routinely measured the heads of her students to identify potential geniuses. However, all of this research had a problem. It did not work. Measuring arms, toes and skulls did not predict academic achievement, criminal conduct or any other psychological predisposition (although it was handy for buying shirts, shoes and hats).

The French scientist Alfred Binet put us on the IQ-testing path we are on today. In 1904, the French government asked Binet to measure the mental ability of school children. Binet thought that intelligence could be calculated by measuring tasks that seemed to require intelligence. He devised a list of things children should know; all he had to do was to ask them if they knew the correct answers. For example, Binet believed that four-year-olds should know their gender; eight-year-olds should be able to count down from twenty to zero; and fifteen-year-olds should be able to repeat a sentence, and so forth. The level at which a child could accomplish these tasks was called the child's *mental age*. The idea was simple: divide the child's mental age by their age in years. The result is the *quotient*. A mental age lower than a chronological age produced a lower IQ score. The test was a success, and soon it was given to so many children that it was considered *standardised,* that is, all results were put onto one common scale so comparisons were possible.

Within a few years, the concept of a standard IQ test swept around the world. It could not have happened at a better time. The First World War was under way and the U.S. Army needed a quick way to determine the ability of the nation's conscripts. The U.S. government used Binet's ideas and devised their own exams, then tested almost two million men. Yet there was a problem: almost half of the men who took the army intelligence tests scored so low they were labelled morons.

The fact that so many able-bodied U.S. soldiers were 'morons' caused a stir. A great debate began about 'ignorant immigrants' entering the country. Of course, the real problem was that many immigrants could not speak English well and they did not understand the test directions. But this did not come to light until after Calvin Coolidge signed the Immigration Restriction Act of 1924. Based largely on U.S. army intelligence test data, this law was designed to stop the flow of 'morons' from coming to America. Thankfully, intelligence testing has improved somewhat in the past eighty years.

While there is still a great deal of debate about race and ethnic bias in intelligence tests, they have been improved and refined in recent years to make them more culturally fair. There has also been a fine-tuning of IQ tests so some are more accurate at particular levels. For example, there are tests now just to distinguish various levels of genius. The IQ test offered on the next page has been developed by geniuses; let's see if you can outsmart them.

TAKING THE TEST

The test you are about to take was developed by Mensa. Mensa is an international organisation whose only selection criterion for joining the club is that members must have an IQ in the top 2 per cent of the population – as measured on a standardised exam. This test will measure several mental abilities, including your verbal and analytical skills and your ability to use logic and solve problems.

Warning: this test is frustrating. You will want to spend more time on the questions than you are allowed. Unlike the other tests in this book, this IQ test is thought to measure some *innate* abilities. When you take the happiness or sexual satisfaction tests, you will know that whatever your score is, you can change your behaviour and improve your score. Generally, this is not the case with intelligence tests. Few people are entirely pleased with their IQ scores.

Take this test at a time when you are comfortable and not distracted. It takes thirty minutes to complete. There are thirty-nine questions. The test will be much more enjoyable and less distracting if you set your watch, an alarm clock or kitchen timer. When you are ready, turn the page and begin. Have fun!

TEST YOURSELF

INSTRUCTIONS

The IQ test you are about to take consists of thirty-nine questions. You will have thirty minutes to complete as many questions as you can. An answer sheet is provided. Mark all your answers on the answer sheet.

Once you are ready with a pencil or pen and a timer, write your name on the answer page. Once thirty minutes are up, you must stop writing.

INTELLIGENCE TEST ANSWER PAGE
Write your answers here

1. _____

2. _____ and _____

3. £ _____

4. a b c d

5. _____

6. _____

7. a b c d

8. _ _ _ _ _ _ _ D

9. _____ is to _____

10. a b c

11. _____

12. a b c

13. a b c d

14. _____ and _____

15. a b c d

16. a b c d

17. a b c d

18. a b c d

19. a b c d

20. _____ and _____

21. £_____

22. a b c d

23. _____

24. a b c d

25. a b c d

26. a b c d e

27. a b c d

28. a b c d

29. _____ and _____

30. a b c d e

31. a b c d

32. a b c d

33. _____ and _____

34. _____

35. _____ is to _____

36. _ _ _ K

37. a b c d

38. a b c d

39. _____ is to _____

STOP

Your Score _____

DO NOT READ THIS PAGE UNTIL YOU ARE READY TO BE TESTED!

1. What number logically follows this series?

$$2, \quad 3, \quad 5, \quad 9, \quad 17, \quad \underline{\hspace{1cm}}$$

2. In the group of words below, which two words are most nearly the opposite in meaning?

Example: **_HEAVY_**, LARGE, FLAT, **_LIGHT_**, BRIGHT

Question: PUNISH, VEX, PINCH, IGNORE, PACIFY, DETERMINE

3. Work out the rule that is used to determine the prices and find the price of the last item.

WATCH	£46
BRACELET	£4
EARRINGS	£10
CHAIN	£6
RING	£ _____

4. Study the four drawings in the top row. Which of the four drawings in the bottom row should appear in the next series?

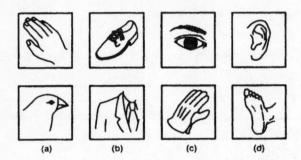

(a) (b) (c) (d)

5. The arrows represent a simple code. What common English word do they spell?

6. In the number square, a rule applies both from top to bottom and left to right. Find the rule and work out the missing number. Note: the example square follows a different rule.

Example: 2   7   9   Question: 6   2   4
             5   4   9   2   ?   0
             7   11   18   4   0   4

7. Which drawing in the bottom row logically comes next in the series that is shown in the top row?

   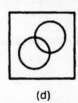

     (a)   (b)   (c)   (d)

8. Complete this analogy by writing one word on the lines, ending with the printed letter.

LEND is to BORROW as HARMONY is to ___ ___ ___ ___ ___ ___ D

9. Which two words in the brackets have the same relation as the two words in the first phrase?

ISLAND is to WATER as (WITHOUT, HYPOTENUSE, CENTRE, DIAGONAL, PERIMETER)

10. If Doris turns either left or right at the stop sign, she will run out of petrol before reaching the filling station. She has already gone too far past the last station to turn around and return to it. She does not see a filling station ahead of her. Therefore:

a. Doris may run out of petrol.

b. Doris will run out of petrol.

c. Doris should not have taken this route.

11. Find the number that logically completes this series.

1,   2,   6,   12,   36,   _____

12. Which building in the bottom row logically comes next in the series that is shown in the top row?

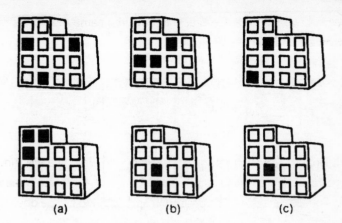

(a)   (b)   (c)

13. M is above N and O. N is above O and below P. Therefore:

   a. M is not above O and P.
   b. O is above N.
   c. P is above O.
   d. O is above P.

14. In the group of words below, which two words are most similar in meaning?

   Example: ***MAT***, LINOLEUM, FLOOR, ***RUG***
   Question: BEAM, LUMP, WOOD, RAY, CHUCKLE, SILVER

15. Which figure in the lower row should appear next in the series of figures in the upper row?

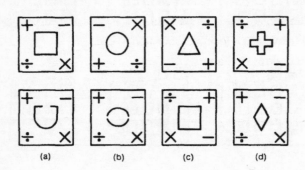

(a)   (b)   (c)   (d)

16. If A × B = 24, B × C = 24, B × D = 48, and C × D = 32, then what does A × B × C × D equal?

a. 480   **b.** 744   **c.** 768   **d.** 824

17. Complete the top series with one of the lettered figures from below.

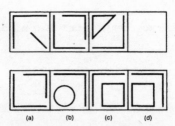

(a)   (b)   (c)   (d)

18. The expression 'Don't throw good money after bad' means:

    a. Take your loss and walk away with it.
    b. Don't gamble; think of the future.
    c. Don't invest in a losing proposition.
    d. Don't borrow to gamble.

19. Sam, Fred, Steve and Joe are weight lifters. Joe can outlift Steve, and Fred can outlift Joe. Steve can outlift Sam. Therefore:

    a. Both Sam and Fred can outlift Joe.
    b. Joe can outlift Sam, but he can't outlift Steve.
    c. Joe can outlift Sam by more than he can outlift Steve.
    d. None of the above is true.

20. Select the two figures in the following that represent mirror images of each other.

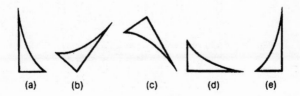

   (a)   (b)   (c)   (d)   (e)

21. Determine what process was followed in arriving at the prices below and find the price of the last item.

SHIRT	£50
TIE	£30
RAINCOAT	£80
SWEATER	£70
BLOUSE	£?

22. Which plate in the bottom row belongs next in the series on the top row?

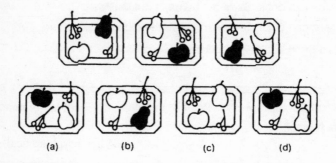

(a) (b) (c) (d)

23. What number logically comes next in this series?

7,   12,   27,   72, _____

24. The old saying 'The good is the enemy of the best' most nearly means:

    a. If you are good, you will best your enemy.

    b. Be good to your best enemy.

    c. Don't accept less than your best.

    d. The good struggle against the best.

25.

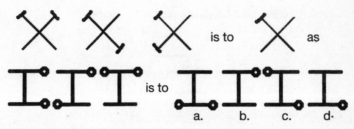

26. Alex, Allan, Carol, Celia and Sharon took intelligence tests. Celia scored higher than Carol, but Allan scored higher than Celia. Carol outscored Alex, but Allan outscored Carol. Sharon scored lower than Allan. Therefore:

    a. Celia scored higher than Alex, but lower than Carol.

    b. Both Alex and Allan outscored Celia.

    c. Sharon scored higher than Carol.

    d. Celia outscored Alex by more than she outscored Carol.

    e. None of the above is definitely true.

27. What number follows logically in this series?

9, 12, 21, 48, _____

a. 69 **b.** 70 **c.** 129 **d.** 144

28. Which one of the letter diagrams in the bottom row can be turned over or rotated to become the same as the top diagram?

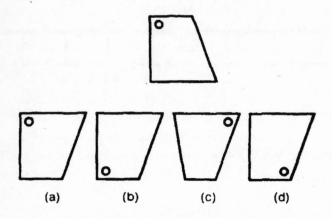

(a)   (b)   (c)   (d)

29. In the group of words below, choose the two words that are most nearly alike in meaning.

TALE, NOVEL, VOLUME, STORY, BOOK

30. If Barbara's daughter is my daughter's mother, what am I to Barbara?

    a. Her grandmother.
    b. Her mother.
    c. Her daughter.
    d. Her granddaughter.
    e. I am Barbara.

31. In a row of four houses, the Whites live next to the Carsons, but not next to the Reeds. If the Reeds do not live next to the Lanes, who are the Lanes' next-door neighbours?

    a. The Whites.
    b. The Carsons.
    c. Both the Whites and the Carsons.
    d. Impossible to tell.

32. WALL is to WINDOW as FACE is to:

    a. SKIN
    b. HAIR
    c. EYE
    d. TEETH

33. Select the two figures in the following series that represent mirror images of each other.

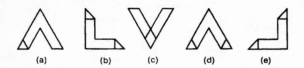

     (a)   (b)   (c)   (d)   (e)

34. What is the next number in this series?

        21,   20,   18,   15,   11,   _____

35. Choose the two words in the brackets that have the same relation as the two words in the first phrase.

EYELID is to EYE as (WINDOW, GLASS, VIEW, CURTAIN, LASH)

36. Complete the following analogy by writing one word on the lines, ending with the printed letter.

SKULL is to BRAIN as SHELL is to _____ _____ _____ K

37. Complete this diagram:

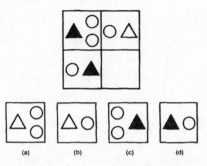

(a)   (b)   (c)   (d)

38. The saying 'A stream cannot rise higher than its source' means:

   a. You decline after achieving your highest level.
   b. Streams of knowledge can't come from high sources.
   c. Your stream of consciousness is highly resourceful.
   d. Your stream of achievement is limited by your background.

39. Choose the two words in the brackets that have the same relation as the two words in the first phrase.

HAT is to HEAD as
(SPOUT, KETTLE, HANDLE, COPPER, LID)

END OF TEST – PLEASE RELAX FOR A COUPLE OF MINUTES.

SCORING YOUR TEST

Okay, you are finished with the test. Many people become discouraged when taking IQ tests. Relax for a moment, then score your results.

The answer key is printed below. Give yourself one point for each answer that agrees with yours. The maximum score is 39. Record your total at the bottom of your answer page (page 8).

1. 33 The difference between successive numbers is double the previous difference OR double each number and subtract one.

2. VEX and PACIFY

3. £36 Price is determined by the first letter of each item. A = £2, B = £4, C = £6, etc.

4. B Aspects of people alternating right, left, right, left. (Only about a third of Mensans got this one right.)

5. NEWS The arrows represent North, East, West and South.

6. 2 The left number in each row minus the middle number equals the right number. Similarly, the top number in each column minus the middle equals the bottom.

7. A The figure rotates anticlockwise. The increments are 45°, 90°, and 135°.

8. DISCORD

9. CENTRE is to PERIMETER

10. A Just because Doris couldn't see a petrol filling station ahead doesn't mean there is not one there.

11. 72 Each succeeding number is multiplied by 2 or 3 alternately.

12. A The dark window on the left goes down one storey on each frame before it starts again at the top. The dark window that starts at the bottom goes up one storey each time and the dark window that starts on the right moves one to the left each time.

13. C

14. BEAM and RAY

15. D The center figure is always solid; the symbols in the corners rotate anti-clockwise.

16. C If $a \times b = 24$, and $c \times d = 32$, then $a \times b \times c \times d = 24 \times 32$ or 768.

17. D The corner angle rotates anticlockwise. The other figure increases its number of lines by one per frame.

18. A

19. C

20. A and E

21. £60 Price is number of letters multiplied by £10.

22. A The apple and pear alternate shading and move anticlockwise. The bunches of cherries rotate clockwise.

23. 207 Each succeeding interval is multiplied by 3, then added to the subsequent number; e.g., $72 - 27 = 45$, $45 \times 3 = 135$, $135 + 72 = 207$.

24. C

25. B The upper dot remains stationary; the lower dot rotates clockwise. It is hidden in the fourth drawing.

26. D

27. C Each increment is multiplied by 3 and added to the following number.

28. B

29. TALE and STORY

30. C

31. A

32. C (99 per cent of Mensans got this one right.)

33. B and E

34. 6 The first number is reduced by 1, the second by 2, the third by 3, etc.

35. CURTAIN is to WINDOW

36. YOLK (Fewer than half of the Mensans got this one right.)

37. A Each square is exactly like its diagonal counterpart, except that the colour of the triangle alternates from black to white.

38. D

39. LID is to KETTLE

UNDERSTANDING YOUR SCORE

Mental ability tests have been studied in such detail that your score on this test can be converted to an IQ score. Use the table below to compare your raw score to the standard IQ score.

Your Score	Your IQ
5 to 11	90 to 109
12 to 16	110 to 119
17 to 22	120 to 129

23 to 28	130 to 139
29 to 34	140 to 149
35 and above	150 and above

WHAT DOES YOUR SCORE MEAN?

What does it mean to have an IQ of 90, or 110, or 130, or whatever your IQ might be? I would like to say that it means you are the same fine person you were when you started this chapter and leave it at that. However, I suspect you may want to learn more.

IQ test scores follow a normal distribution or 'bell curve'. The average IQ is always 100. IQ scores can be between 0 and 200, but it is almost impossible to measure people at the highest and lowest levels. The figure below illustrates how IQ scores are distributed and how specific score ranges have been labelled in the past.

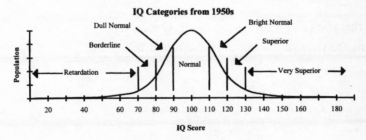

Distribution of IQ Test Categories

YOUR SCORE *Score of 90–109*

Your intelligence as measured on this test is about average. You have tested in the 'normal' range. You are probably brighter than half of the population. Fifty per cent of the population have an IQ in this category. A score of 90 places you in the 40th percentile. A score of 109 propels you to the 60th percentile.

Score of 110–119

Your intelligence as measured on this test is better than average. You are probably brighter than 70 per cent of the population. You are 'bright normal'. Sixteen per cent of the population belong in this category. A score of 110 places you above the 60th percentile. An IQ of 119 puts you past the 75th percentile.

Score of 120–129

Your intelligence as measured on this test is great. You are probably brighter that 85 per cent of the population. Your IQ is in the 'superior' category. Just under 7 per cent of the population test in this category. A score of 120 puts your IQ at the 77th percentile while a score of 129 pushes you just shy of the 90th percentile.

Score of 130–139

Your intelligence as measured on this test is excellent. You are probably brighter than 93 per cent of the population. Your score identifies your intelligence as 'very superior'. An IQ of 139 places you in the top five percent, or 95th percentile.

Score of 140–149

Your intelligence as measured on this test is superb. You are probably brighter than 98 per cent of the population. Your score identifies your intelligence as 'genius'. If you scored 148 or above, you may want to apply to Mensa, the organisation for people with IQs in the top 2 per cent. You were probably insufficiently stimulated at school.

Score of 150 and Above

Your intelligence as measured on this test indicates that you are one of the brightest people in the country. You are in the brightest fraction of the population. Your score identifies your intelligence as 'genius'. You probably found school boring. Perhaps your peers could not relate to you intellectually.

**IF YOU SCORED ABOVE 150 AND PUT YOUR MIND TO IT,
YOU COULD DEVISE A BETTER TEST!**

How Do You Compare?

Now that you know *your* intelligence quotient, let's see how you compare to other groups who have taken IQ tests. These studies are organised in the stages of life.

IQ IN CHILDHOOD

WERE YOU A BIG BABY?

Although it sounds a little as though we are weighing brains again, there is something to the notion that birth weights are linked to IQs. We have known for some years that small babies tend to have lower IQs, but that was chalked up to poor maternal health, smoking and socioeconomic disadvantages. But a 2001 study of 3,500 seven-year-olds showed there is a link between birth weight and IQ, even among 'normal'-sized babies (4 to 10 lbs.) Epidemiologists at Columbia University and the New York Academy of Medicine learned that for about every two pounds of birth weight, boys will have an IQ 4.6 points higher than their thinner siblings. For unknown reasons this effect is not as great with girls. Still, their IQ is up almost 3 points for every couple of pounds heavier they were at birth.

WERE YOU A TALL CHILD?

If you were a tall child, chances are you are more intelligent than someone who was shorter. Paediatrician Darrell Wilson studied the link between height and IQ. He surveyed fourteen thousand children. After taking variables like birth order, family size, family income and race into account, a clear trend emerged: taller children tended to have higher IQs. Wilson thought that perhaps height-based expectations could account for the difference. That is, taller children are treated as if they are more mature. So, I suppose it is okay to marry a big baby.

WERE YOU THE TEACHER'S PET?

If you were the teacher's pet, you must be a smarty-pants. Professor Kathryn Wentzel investigated a host of variables influencing eleven- to fourteen-year-olds for her article 'Does Being Good Make the Grade?' published in the *Journal of Educational Psychology*. The old stereotype of 'teacher's pet' is alive and well. Wentzel found that IQ was significantly correlated with the following goody-two-shoes type behaviours: sharing, cooperating with others, getting good grades, good attendance and, of course, teacher preference.

HOW DID YOU DO IN SCHOOL?

You don't have to be a genius to excel in school; just look below . . .

IQ and EDUCATION

100	Mean of the population.
105	Mean of high school graduates.
115	Mean of college graduates.
125	Mean of Ph.D. and M.D. recipients.

IQ IN ADULTHOOD

HOW IS YOUR DRIVING?

In 1991, there was an interesting study of accident-prone drivers in China. The authors studied drivers who had caused three or more accidents and compared them to drivers with clean records. The safe drivers were similar to the accident-prone drivers in age, sex, marital status, education, occupation, kind of vehicle, driving experience, eyesight, hearing, even arm and leg length. You name it, they matched it. The idea behind this experiment was to isolate the one difference between the two groups, which was IQ. They found that on tests that measure *performance* IQ (such as finishing an unfinished drawing and arranging blocks in a meaningful way), the accident-prone drivers scored much lower than their matched counterparts.

ARE MENSA MEMBERS NARCISSISTIC?

Mensa is an international organisation whose selection criterion for joining the club is that members must have an IQ of at least 148. As long as your IQ is in the top 2 per cent you can join the group, regardless of your achievements or character. Announcing your Mensa membership is a little like telling the world that you are a smarty-pants. Because of this, a popular stereotype exists that Mensans are narcissistic. To test this, a couple of psychologists gave Mensan and non-Mensan university students a questionnaire that measures narcissism. Guess what? The stereotype is wrong. Narcissism scores were not much different between the groups. It appears that individuals enrolled in Mensa are no more self-absorbed than college students.

DO YOU FANTASIZE DURING SEX?

If you are a bright woman, there is a good chance that you actively fantasize during sex. Sex psychologist Dr Manfred DeMartino interviewed more than three hundred women in Mensa. In his book *Sex and the Intelligent Woman,* he claims that the most common fantasies for women with IQs over 130 are sex with someone other than a current partner, group sex, acting out scenes from pornographic books and films, and exposing oneself.

DO YOU USE CONTRACEPTIVES?

Just over half of all adolescents in the United States become sexually active in their high school years. Two-thirds of these do not regularly use contraception, resulting in more than one million unwanted pregnancies each year. In 1991, a trio of paediatricians looked into this problem. They divided volunteers of girls aged thirteen to sixteen into three groups:

1. Those who are sexually active and using contraception.
2. Those who are sexually active and not using contraception.
3. Those who are not sexually active.

They found that group 1 had the highest IQs and the most knowledge about contraception. Group 2 had the lowest IQs and the least knowledge about contraceptive practices, and group 3 scored in the middle of both measures.

ARE YOU A RACIST?

American professors Drs Daniel Lapsley and Robert Enright went to a university in the southern United States known for its conservative values. They gave students an IQ test and a test measuring racial prejudice. Sure enough, the correlation was there: less-intelligent students are more prejudiced.

WHAT IS YOUR SPOUSE'S INTELLIGENCE?

Husbands and wives tend to have the same IQs. Is it due to:

1. Initially choosing a partner with similar intelligence?
2. IQs becoming similar during marriage because of shared mental stimulation and diet (what psychologists call *convergence*)?
3. Dissimilar couples getting divorced?

A certain amount of convergence takes place throughout married life, but only for 'plastic' variables (those characteristics that are more easily changed), like smoking, socialising and alcohol consumption. Intelligence has genetic roots and therefore it cannot be changed easily. The answer, according to University of Cambridge anthropologist Nick Mascie-Taylor, is number 1. People originally choose partners who are thought to have an intelligence like their own.

IS YOUR MAN SUPERIOR?

William James, a social biologist, put forward a politically incorrect argument for 'Husband Superiority'. He says it is commonplace for bright single women to complain that they do not want to appear too intelligent, whereas men rarely make this objection. James reasons that like height and age, spouses select one another based on male intellectual superiority. While there are plenty of numbers to demonstrate that most women marry men who are taller and slightly older, does this pattern also hold true for intelligence?

Whether you like it or not, men and women do tend to form pairs where the woman is slightly less intelligent. A study that measured the mental abilities of almost two hundred British couples found that husbands were on average brighter than their wives – but by a mere 2 IQ points.

By the way, women prefer men who are taller than themselves by a whopping 6.7 inches, whereas men prefer women who are only 4.5 inches shorter.

HOW MANY CHILDREN DO YOU HAVE?

On average, the brighter you are, the fewer children you will have. Dr Robert Retherford, former president of the East West Population Institute, found this interesting information while studying over ten thousand Americans for eighteen years. By the time respondents turned thirty-five, people with higher IQs had significantly fewer children. The effect was particularly pronounced in men. Retherford suggests that because brighter people stay in school longer, have more interests outside of family life and tend to know more about contraception, they have fewer opportunities to make babies. The effect is greater in men because many high-IQ women in the study chose marriage and children over continuing their education.

DO YOU WEAR GLASSES?

You know the old stereotype of the nerd – a genius with glasses? Well, two Israeli ophthalmologists tested over 150,000 military recruits. They discovered that the stereotype is true. There is a strong correlation between nearsightedness and high IQ.

DO YOU HAVE LARGE BREASTS?

If you do, then it does not matter what your IQ is – at least when you first meet someone. Regardless of your actual IQ, research has found that women whose bust size was thirty-seven inches and bigger were perceived as stupid, incompetent and immoral at first impression by both men *and* women. Conversely, women with smaller busts, that is, less than thirty-four inches, were perceived as more intelligent, competent and moral than their more endowed sisters.

HAVE YOU EVER COMMITTED A CRIME?

And speaking of the immoral, there is an immense interest in learning about criminal personalities. On average, people who commit crimes have below average intelligence. But the picture is not that clear. We do know that people who lack the verbal ability to deal with life's problems may act out their anger and frustration. Delinquents with lower IQs are drawn to impulsive crimes that produce instant gratification, whereas high-IQ delinquents prefer to plan out their crimes and have the savvy to wait for deferred gratification. We also know that low-IQ delinquents are most likely to commit violent crimes compared to their more intellectual cell mates. This is because violent crimes generally require less planning and are more spontaneous. The smarter crooks tend to commit property crimes, which require greater planning and forethought, but offer potentially more valuable payoffs.

DO YOU SMOKE MARIJUANA?

Studies have shown that frequent marijuana use can lower intelligence. But can this decrease be reversed? Dr James Smith and his colleagues asked chronic marijuana users to participate in a smoking cessation study. The participants he selected were twenty-four to forty years old, employed and married. But they had been hooked on dope for an average of thirteen years and were smoking at least three joints a day.

First, Dr Smith measured his volunteers' IQs. Then he led each person into a room in which there was a table covered with marijuana, rolling papers, matches, lighters and paraphernalia. (However, the psychoactive ingredient in the marijuana, THC, had been removed.) Subjects were allowed to smoke what they could, but they received an electric shock every time they reached for anything.

On the second day they were asked to 'groom' the marijuana by removing seeds and stems. Again the volunteers were given shocks as they groomed. On the third day the subjects were told to smoke rapidly – one puff every six seconds – without putting the marijuana down. However, they received a shock every time they took a puff.

By the end of the five days of this treatment, every volunteer reported abstinence. Three weeks later, Smith tested their IQs again. The results: the average IQ went up a staggering six points! Virtually every subject's IQ increased. It seems that the cognitive deficits created by marijuana are reversible to some extent. Incidentally, one year after the shock treatment, over 90 per cent of the volunteers recontacted remained drug free.

WHAT IS INTELLIGENCE WITHOUT KNOWLEDGE?

It is said that 'the first line of defence for a country is a well-informed citizenry'. It's possible to have high intelligence, but little knowledge. For example, a survey of twelve hundred randomly selected Americans found that well over half could not name one Supreme Court justice! However, don't despair. Almost 60 per cent easily named the Three Stooges. And they say kids don't learn nothin' in skool. Nyuk, nyuk, nyuk!

DO YOU REMEMBER THINGS FROM LONG AGO?

Two British researchers studied hundreds of people aged fifty-four to eighty-three. They measured IQ and then the clarity of the individuals' first memories. They found that the brightest people could remember when they were about three years old. Older people of average intelligence recalled when they were almost four years old. And the lowest IQ seniors could not remember events from before their fifth birthdays. These earliest memories were related to their IQs, not to their age.

WANT TO INCREASE YOUR IQ?

For more than a century, psychologists have been using reaction times to help measure intelligence. A group of psychologists tested the reaction time of more than one hundred cigarette smokers. The smokers made decisions and pressed buttons as quickly as they could. Each was then given one cigarette to smoke and then tested again. The result: a significant improvement. The report states, 'Smoking of a cigarette by a smoker under naturalistic conditions improves the performance of the smoker on an IQ-related task.' Of course, this study was funded by a cigarette manufacturer.

Well, if you are not keen on smoking, try chewing gum. That's right, gum can make you smarter! In 2002, two British neuroscientists divided a group of seventy-five volunteers into three groups.

One group got a stick of gum, another was told to pretend to chew gum and the third just sat in a room. Each subject had three minutes to chew, pretend to chew or sit, and then they were given a twenty-five-minute test.

The results were clear – you can double your pleasure, double your fun and remember 35 per cent more after a good chew. Why? Our brains may become better memory stores due to increased blood flow to the brain (chewing gum raises the heartbeat by three beats per minute), and gum causes a surge of insulin because of the mouthwatering appeal of a snack. The brain is loaded with insulin receptors in areas that are known to promote learning and memory.

2
CREATIVITY

The artist is a receptacle for emotions that come from all over the place: from the sky, from the earth, from a scrap of paper, from a passing shape, from a spider's web. PABLO PICASSO

Creativity is what separates humans from all other creatures. While intelligence is useful, creativity adds colour, texture and sound to the fabric of humanity. In fact, intelligence without creativity is like a yacht without a rudder. As a species we are fabulous creators. We demonstrate our abilities by pursuing science, painting, music, architecture, psychology, humour and countless other activities. But are all humans creative? Or, more pointedly, how creative are you? In this chapter we will examine personality aspects of the creative, measure your creative powers and suggest ways to nurture them.

WHAT IS CREATIVITY?

Let's begin by taking a step back to a time when creativity was not thought of as a human trait. In every known primitive culture, creativity was considered to be in the hands of supreme beings. From the Ancient Greeks to the native American Navajo to the San bushmen of the Kalahari Desert, every culture has described its origins, existence and surroundings in elaborate stories. In these myths, people were the humble subjects of all-powerful creatures. Humans were helpless. Mysterious deities controlled the beasts, the oceans and the sky. Creation myths were handed down by generations as part of culture. It is ironic that these detailed stories of helpless humans are proof of how wonderfully creative we are.

But how do we begin to create? And why? To create, you must produce something that would not otherwise exist in nature. For example, although berries, fingers and bamboo are natural, it takes creativity to use these items to make paint, maths and music. By learning about the natural world, blending information and using it in novel ways, we are being creative. This is how men and women have developed richly complicated modern cultures.

For creativity to flourish, however, there must be a distinct set of symbols. We use symbols for language, maths, physics, art, music and countless other creative endeavours. On a societal scale, creativity exists by mastering the symbols of a discipline and arranging them into new patterns, like a composer creating music.

Or like an architect, we blend the knowledge of many disciplines to design a modern skyscraper. On a more personal level, being creative may involve breaking some old habits and bringing a fresh approach to everyday activities. In either case, the outcome is something both unique and useful, something that makes life richer.

CREATIVE PEOPLE

It is well known that there have been people whose creative contributions have changed the world. The Curies, da Vinci, Shakespeare, Gandhi, Mozart and many other exceptionally dedicated individuals have become so committed to their work that they have changed their realm forever. Their creative contributions, though at first considered radical and sometimes crazy, have redefined their field of study. What else do these extraordinarily creative people have in common? Let's explore the 'creative character'.

THE CREATIVE CHARACTER
What makes a creative character? Here are the eight ingredients:

1. Taking Risks

> *Painting is freedom. If you jump, you might fall*
> *on the wrong side of the rope. But if you are not*

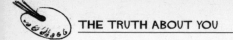

> *willing to take the risk of breaking your neck,*
> *what good is it? You don't jump at all.* PICASSO

As humans, we are born with two conflicting sets of instructions. First of all, we must be conservative. The innate desire to find food and shelter and to conserve energy in preparation for emergencies has allowed our species to survive relentlessly through the ages. Boring, you say? Right! What is life without a bit of daring? Which brings us to the other side of humans, the expansive side: the part of us that says, *Explore! Take risks! Dare to be different!* Creative people are apt to heed this call.

2. Standing Alone

New ideas are risky and so is standing apart from the crowd. Many creative personalities are misunderstood. At one time, Picasso's cubist paintings were widely regarded as worthless. They were openly ridiculed by critics and satirised, compelling the artist to keep many works hidden away. For the most creative, recognition is often preceded by rejection. Humans like convention; they like to be comfortable. Creative individuals dare to be different; they are willing to stand alone for their beliefs.

3. Acquiring Knowledge

No matter how brilliant you might be, you cannot create without a knowledge of your subject. Ideas do not come out of thin air; they come from combining old knowledge in new ways. An engineer must know the properties of metals just as a mother must know what will delight her children to make something special. The most creative among us master their fields and then gather knowledge from a extensive array of topics. They fuse the details of different disciplines and create something new. For example, I read of an inventor who fills a fish bowl full of slips of paper. On each sheet she writes one fact about an object or human behaviour. Then, every morning, she dips her hand in the bowl and chooses two slips, then spends the day mulling over what new invention could be made with these two varied pieces of knowledge.

4. Analysing Your Work

The creative don't produce works indiscriminately. They constantly question and analyse what they have done. Since our time to create is limited to one lifetime, it is important for us to quickly discern the good works from the bad. The sooner you dismiss the bad, the sooner you can create something of quality. This is often why painters number their works: they are a series of research projects. Each one is judged and critiqued by the artist so that the creative progress can be forged.

5. Dreaming

It is common for original ideas to come to us when we least expect them. You hear people say, 'It just popped into my head' or, 'It came to me in a dream'. Whether while driving, jogging or sleeping soundly, creative ideas often come when our mind is in repose. This is when the subconscious allows us to transcend boundaries and break our own rules. In every discipline, people use restful interludes to enhance inspiration. Sometimes a simple, short walk is all that is needed to get those creative juices flowing.

6. Loving Your Work

Being creative is hard work. The promise of fame and fortune is rarely a source of motivation. Creative people pursue their fields with or without pay or recognition; it is simply their favourite thing to do. It is a labour of love. Those who have a passion for their pastime are the most creative.

7. Implementing Ideas

It is a misconception that creative people are only dreamers. Although dreaming is indeed a part of the creative character, it is more important to be practical. A sculptor's creative vision amounts to little more than whimsy until he or she takes hammer in hand and begins chipping rock. Creative ideas are worthless unless you can *make them happen*.

8. Finding an Audience

Like Picasso, Vincent Van Gogh was a creative genius. He mastered his field, loved his work and produced vast amounts of original material. Yet he died unrecognised, penniless and mad. Unfortunately, he was about a century ahead of his audience. It's a cruel reality, but without acceptance from an audience, creativity may slip away unnoticed.

A Brief History of Creativity Testing: How We Got Here

The study of creativity began in earnest in the United States in the 1950s. World War II was over and the country was getting back on its feet. The economy was booming and a new era of design and manufacturing began. Wild discoveries in the uses of plastics were being made, American car manufacturers enjoyed a golden age, steel and glass box architecture pushed the nation's skyscrapers to new heights and the launch of *Sputnik* in 1957 sparked the U.S. space programme into action. The country was looking for bright, creative engineers to meet the public's demand for new and better products.

In that same year at Purdue University, graduate student Doug Harris, along with his professor Chuck Lawshe, realised the need to identify creative individuals. Harris and Lawshe worked together to create what is now known as the Purdue Engineer's Creativity Test. The test is good for several reasons: it is fun, it is cross-cultural and it is brief. The test was originally written to identify creative engineers. However, it has been used extensively in other fields. You are fortunate to have a chance to complete this quiz, as the Engineer's Creativity Test is a seminal work. Believe me, in the history of personality testing, this is a biggie.

Now, if you are one of those wordsmiths who roll your eyes at spatial tasks but have a knack for language, fear not – I have a test for you as well. Around the same time that our Purdue friends were developing their test, two psychologists from the University of Michigan had a different notion of creativity. Sarnoff and Martha Mednick believed that finding relationships between remote ideas spelled creativity. They reported that successful poets, writers, scientists and mathematicians took disparate ideas and linked them together. For example, when given the words *gold, stool* and *tender,* a creative mind can search for a relationship between these concepts. Here, the word *bar* provides the creative link: gold bar, barstool and bartender. The Mednicks took this idea, developed quite a fun test and called it the Remote Associates Test (RAT). I have sampled some items from the RAT and refer to it here as the Wordsmith's Creativity Test. We will start with the wordsmith's test, then try rocket science.

TAKING THE WORDSMITH'S CREATIVITY TEST

Take this test at a time when you are comfortable and not distracted. This test measures how well you can form links between

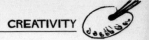
unrelated ideas. It is difficult: most people solve only half of the twenty questions. But there is a thrill after getting a question right. There is no time constraint. It may take you twenty to forty minutes to take a crack at the twenty questions.

TEST YOURSELF

INSTRUCTIONS

For each of the following sets of three words, find the fourth word that is related to the other three.

For example, what word is related to:

Paint   Summer   Boat _____

The answer is *house,* because it forms the words house paint, summer house, house boat.

Here is another example:

Stool   Powder   Ball _____

The answer in this example is *foot*: footstool, foot powder, football. Please note that not all answers form word blends; some associations are with concepts that the word may create in your mind.

When you are ready, turn the page and begin. Have fun!

WORDSMITH'S CREATIVITY TEST

1.	Widow	Bite	Monkey	_____
2.	Bald	Screech	Emblem	_____
3.	Walker	Main	Sweeper	_____
4.	Blood	Music	Cheese	_____
5.	Chamber	Staff	Box	_____
6.	Lick	Sprinkle	Mines	_____
7.	Bass	Complex	Sleep	_____
8.	Chocolate	Fortune	Tin	_____
9.	Mouse	Sharp	Blue	_____
10.	Envy	Golf	Beans	_____
11.	Athletes	Web	Rabbit	_____
12.	Board	Magic	Death	_____
13.	Lapse	Vivid	Elephant	_____
14.	Room	Blood	Salts	_____
15.	Puss	Tart	Spoiled	_____
16.	Stop	Petty	Sneak	_____
17.	Inch	Deal	Peg	_____
18.	Note	Dive	Chair	_____
19.	Shopping	Washer	Picture	_____
20.	Sore	Shoulder	Sweat	_____

END OF TEST

A sample of items from S. A. Mednick and M. T. Mednick, *Examiner's Manual: Remote Associates Test Form 1*. Boston: Houghton Mifflin, 1967. Used with permission.

SCORING YOUR TEST

Okay, take a breather for a moment. You probably struggled to realise some answers; don't worry. Scoring the test is easy. The answer key is printed below. You will certainly have a few *aha!* moments as you read the key. Give yourself one point for each correct answer.

1 Spider	**8** Cookie	**15** Sour
2 Eagle	**9** Cheese	**16** Thief
3 Street	**10** Green	**17** Square
4 Blue	**11** Foot	**18** High
5 Music	**12** Black	**19** Window
6 Salt	**13** Memory	**20** Cold
7 Deep	**14** Bath	

To convert your score to a percentile, use the chart below.

YOUR SCORE	PERCENTILE	CONCLUSION
6 or less	10th	
8	20th	*A Tad Creative*
9	30th	
10	40th	
11	50th	*Average*
13	60th	
14	70th	
15	80th	*Highly Creative*
16 or more	90th	

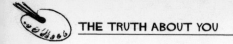

WHAT DOES YOUR SCORE MEAN?

First of all, if you did not score as well as you wanted, don't fret. Even if you performed poorly, you may still be creative in ways not measured by this test. Also, you can take some solace in this: those who score lower on this test tend to have *better* grades in school.

YOUR SCORE

Scores Below 9. The Works of Emily Dickinson Are Safe

You probably found this quiz frustrating. You were unable to find as many links between the word triplets as the average American. Some of the terms may have been unfamiliar to you. Don't worry – you can improve this skill. Write your own questions and answers. Try to think of novel links between your job and other concepts like painting, building, music and nature. Open the curtains around your mind that keep it from wandering. Think of the roots of various words, how to make them into puns and what words rhyme with them. Have fun with it.

Scores Between 10 and 13. A Budding Wordsmith!

You have some creative tendencies, but you fall somewhere in the middle of this scale. Your score is about average for a well-educated person. It is time to stretch your creativity muscles. Give yourself a ten-minute workout every day and you will perform even better. Think of unusual links between words, practise making puns, try to

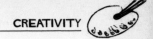

mix ideas from the arts into your work life. Check out the creativity-enhancing ideas at the end of this chapter. By thinking of words and ideas in new ways you will become more innovative, inventive and inspired.

Scores Above 14. You Are Shakespeare in Love!

Your creativity could give the Bard a run for his money! You are a quick wordsmith and, probably, an amusing person to have around. People want you at parties; you are a poet and a wit. Your verbal creativity skills are in the top third of originality. Keep on working those inventive brain cells. Try the creativity-enhancing exercises at the end of the chapter.

TAKING THE PURDUE CREATIVITY TEST FOR ENGINEERS

Now that you have learned about your verbal skills, let's test your ingenuity using objects. Before you start, here are some hints: you can improve your score on the engineer's creativity test by keeping these three elements of inventiveness in mind:

1. **Flexibility** is the number of different types of ideas you can generate. In other words, it is not enough to generate many ideas: to be creative, the ideas you construct must be significantly different.

For example, if you saw a drawing of a nail, you might report that it could be used as a nail, a bolt and a door latch. These would be considered ideas with low flexibility, because they all are tools for connecting objects. Another reader whose responses included a lightning rod, a balloon popper and an axle would be considered more flexible. These ideas come from using three of the nail's properties: its ability to conduct electricity, its point and its cylindrical shape.

2. **Fluency** is the number of ideas generated within one topic. For example, if a circular object were thought to be a coin, the respondent might list a pound, a Euro, a shilling or a centavo. This would show fluency.

3. **Originality** is the number of times that ideas on rare categories are reported. If you can suggest how the nail could create world peace, I suspect you would be the only one to provide an answer in that category. That would be extremely original.

Take this test at a time when you are comfortable and not distracted. This test is both fun and frustrating. It measures your creativity and gives you a chance to invent. But there is a time constraint. You only have sixteen minutes to jot down your ideas on eight drawings. You may get annoyed because you know that you can come up with more answers, but time allows only two minutes per picture. Set a timer or get a friend to watch the clock. When you are ready, turn the page and begin. Have fun!

TEST YOURSELF

INSTRUCTIONS

The purpose of this test is to determine how creatively you think. The test you are about to take consists of eight drawings like the example shown below. You will have sixteen minutes to list as many possible uses as you can for these objects. Write your responses on the lines beneath the drawing. Mark all your answers on the answer sheet.

EXAMPLE

1. *A rolling pin.*
2. *A vase.*
3. *A camera lens or telescope.*
4. *A section of pipe.*
5. *A candle holder.*
6. *A bulb planter.*
7. *A press to make sausages.*
8. *Insulator for electrical wires.*
9. *Gun barrel.*
10. *A paint roller.*
11. *Air nozzle for blowing up balloons.*
12. *A whistle.*

ENGINEER'S CREATIVITY TEST, PAGE 1

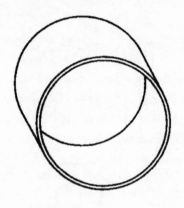

_____

_____

_____

_____

_____

_____

_____

ENGINEER'S CREATIVITY TEST, PAGE 2

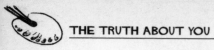
ENGINEER'S CREATIVITY TEST, PAGE 3

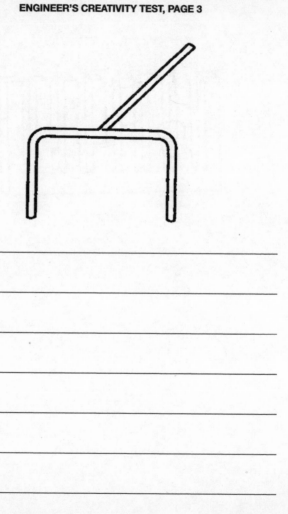

_____

_____

_____

_____

_____

_____

_____

ENGINEER'S CREATIVITY TEST, PAGE 4

_____

_____

_____

_____

_____

_____

_____

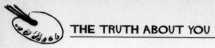

ENGINEER'S CREATIVITY TEST, PAGE 5

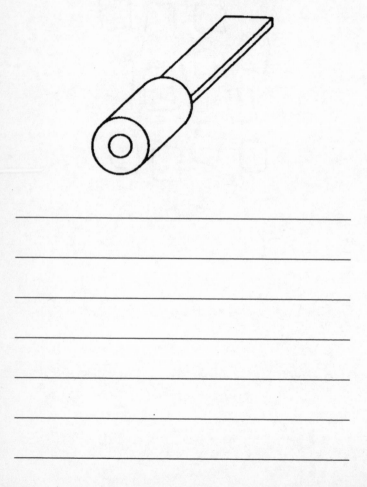

_____

_____

_____

_____

_____

_____

_____

ENGINEER'S CREATIVITY TEST, PAGE 6

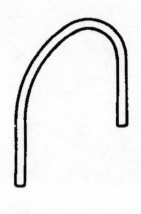

_____

_____

_____

_____

_____

_____

_____

ENGINEER'S CREATIVITY TEST, PAGE 7

_____

_____

_____

_____

_____

_____

_____

_____

ENGINEER'S CREATIVITY TEST, PAGE 8

_____

_____

_____

_____

_____

_____

END OF TEST

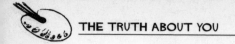

Scoring Your Test

To begin, look at your answers methodically and draw a line through any items that are too general. For instance, if one of your responses could be applied to several of the pictures rather than just one, then that answer should be eliminated. Next, omit answers that are simply different names for the same thing. For example, if you wrote *paint scraper* and *putty knife* for the fifth drawing, leave only one. Finally, total your remaining responses to get your score. Give yourself one point for each answer. To convert your score to a percentile, use the chart below.

YOUR SCORE	PERCENTILE	CONCLUSION
16 or less	10th	
19	20th	*A Smidgen of*
22	30th	*Imagination*
25	40th	
28	50th	*Average*
30	60th	
33	70th	
36	80th	*Ingenious and Inventive*
41 or more	90th	

WHAT DOES YOUR SCORE MEAN?

First of all, don't worry if you did not do well. Even if you performed poorly, you may still be creative in ways not measured by this test. As mentioned earlier, each test is designed to measure a specific facet of creativity. Since this one deals with flexibility rather than fluency or originality, you may have scored better had we focused on a different area.

Also, it is important to note that the above percentiles were taken from the test scores of engineers. Had you been competing with peers within your own profession, you may have fared differently.

Finally, even if you are not particularly creative, there is no need to worry. You can increase your creative skills. It is more important that you desire to be *your* best.

YOUR SCORE
Scores Between 0 and 22. Houston, We Have a Problem!
If you scored in this range, you probably found this test to be immensely frustrating. You saw fewer uses for the various objects than the average test taker. You may have run out of time or simply quit on an object that seemed particularly strange or unfamiliar. Don't worry. Get those mental juices flowing by going back to the test and taking your time with each item. Try to take some risks. Remember, the key is to be flexible, so drop the rigid blinders that block your mind from wandering. Try turning the pictures upside down,

pretend they are soft-sided balloons, or made from paper. Consider the fantastic.

Sit down with your friends or family and brainstorm together. Learn your weaknesses from the ideas of others. For instance, if your thoughts were restricted to human uses while your young daughter saw dog toys, learn from her. Draw your own objects, swap them and quiz each other for creativity. If you feel you are more fluent than flexible, change the rules: say that your object must be used as a marital aid, to create music or to rear sheep. If you still struggle finding uses for odd objects, focus on the Wordsmith's Creativity Test. Perhaps you are verbally gifted.

Scores Between 23 and 30. You Could Improve Some of da Vinci's Inventions.

Not bad! You could give Leonardo a run for his money – if you apply your skills. You scored in the average area for spatial creative abilities. You can either rest on your resourceful laurels or get up and run a bit. Make yourself aware of your creative abilities and put them to work on a daily basis. Whether you are more flexible on the job, trying your talents with an artistic hobby, or just solving the brainteasers in your local paper, you can both stretch and improve your creative powers. Think of your creativity as a set of muscles that you can pump to awe-inspiring proportions or let go to flab from lack of use.

One fun way to exercise your creativity muscle is to play originality games with friends. As mentioned above, get a group of friends together and ask each person to draw their own quiz objects, swap them and test each other for creativity. Life gets more interesting when you use your creativity – whether to help and inspire others or to please yourself. But by all means, use it!

Scores over 30. Roll Over, Beethoven!

You are innovative, resourceful and inspired. You are able to think quickly and imaginatively even under pressure. You are a problem solver and are not afraid to experiment with new ideas. All of these qualities make you a valuable participant in the workplace and with friends. You are the kind of person who folks love to have around when there are problems to be solved. Practice will make perfect, and you can further improve your creativity with regular exercises. Read the answer categories above for helpful suggestions. Further recommendations are made at the end of the chapter.

HOW DO YOU COMPARE?

Now that you know your creativity score, let's see how you compare to others who have taken creativity tests. We will begin by taking a general look at the complexity of the creative personality, then view creativity as it applies to work and home life.

DO YOU HAVE A CREATIVE PERSONALITY?

Creative people are complex. Their personalities move from one extreme to another, and they seldom end up in the middle. Hungarian-born creativity expert Mihaly Csikszentmihalyi (pronounced 'chick-SENT-me-high-ee') interviewed almost one hundred exceptionally creative individuals and found some basic paradoxes that exist in the truly creative.

Do These Describe You?

1. Creative people tend to be highly intelligent, but they often see the world with childlike naïveté.
2. Creative people tend to be playful and irresponsible, yet extremely disciplined and persistent with their work.
3. Creative people interchange reality with fantasy. Their work often reflects a spontaneous leap from the real to the imaginative.
4. Creative people tend to fluctuate between introversion and extroversion. While most of us are either one or the other, the creative are often introverted while deep in thought and extroverted while performing or explaining their ideas.
5. Creative people transcend gender roles. Creative men can freely express sensitive, gentle behaviour and may be extremely focused on their families. Often, creative women can be more aggressive and assertive than is customary for their culture.
6. Creative people know all the rules, yet they are rebellious. They seek out the rules and boundaries of their domain and then selectively deconstruct them. In the arts, creative people will break the

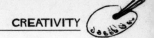

rules and introduce taboo subjects. The most inventive of us break with tradition and ask, 'What would happen if this fact was false?'

7. Creative people oscillate between great joy when they are immersed in their work and incredible melancholy when criticised. The life of the creative is hard. They are like a turtle without a shell, happy when working in their world, but sensitive and unable to protect themselves when attacked.

DO YOU HAVE A MESSY DESK?

If you keep a messy desk, it does not matter how original you are – people will think you are creative anyway. Psychologist Sarah Sitton showed photographs to University of Texas students. The photographs were of offices that featured either a messy desk or a clean one. Each photo also included either a man in a suit sitting at the desk or an unoccupied office. The messy desk was not just cluttered, it was a real mess with over one hundred items on it. The clean desk was tidy with just three items arranged on it. The students were then asked to rate the personality of each worker.

The results show:

People Who Have Messy Desks Are Seen as More:	People Who Have Tidy Desks Are Seen as More:
Creative	Intelligent
Kind	Ambitious
Active	Calm
Social	Organized

Interestingly, the subject of the photograph was perceived as less creative when he was shown in the office. So if you really want to look creative, keep your desk cluttered, and don't go near it.

DO YOU ENJOY TELLING JOKES?

While you are not working at your messy desk, you should be hanging around the water cooler telling jokes. In a study similar to the above, a group of researchers asked students to rate how original and creative joke writers were. The result: the funnier the joke, the more creative its author is perceived.

Now, there is more to this concept than you think. Not only will people believe you are more creative if you tell jokes, you probably *are* more creative.

It seems that both telling jokes and being creative involve taking risks. (See the first ingredient of the creative character.) For a joke to be funny it has to have an unexpected ending. It must be unusual. The same goes for creativity.

ARE YOU LONELY?

Common wisdom suggests that loneliness and creativity go hand in hand, that somehow creative people are unable to form friendships. They withdraw from emotional involvement with others and are prone to isolation. That is, they can't make friends so they get lonely. Fortunately, this is a myth, according to an interesting study conducted on adolescents. It seems teenagers are most likely to feel

the angst of loneliness and the burst of creativity. But just because they can happen around the same time in life does not make them *cause* each other. It turns out that the most creative teenagers are also the ones who are least lonely. So why the myth? It could be that creative individuals who seek solace in their work are mistakenly seen as unsociable. Another possibility is that we view lonely people as more creative than they really are.

CAN YOU BUY CREATIVITY?

It is widely believed that if you reward someone for being creative, creativity will diminish. Several studies have demonstrated that children who are praised for being creative will try hard, work more and produce more, but their work becomes of lower quality. The problem is that people who get rewarded for being creative unwittingly change; instead of working on projects for intrinsic enjoyment, many end up doing it for the money. As a result, creativity diminishes. But there is one thing that money can't buy, and that is *persistence*. Being creative requires hard work and there are long periods of frustration and wasted effort. People will put up with disappointment if they are paid for it. Hence, rewarding people for sticking to a task has a greater effect on creativity than paying for the product itself.

ARE YOU A RUNNER?

If you run, you are probably more creative than your sedentary colleagues. Two physical education professors learned this after studying two groups of students. One group was given a health lecture twice a week for twenty minutes, while the other group ran for twenty minutes twice a week.

All students were given three creativity tests before the classes and again at the end of sixteen weeks. The students who ran regularly scored as significantly more creative. Incidentally, runners improved most on a test similar to the Purdue one.

ARE YOU A DREAMER?

Creative people have wild minds, even at rest. The most creative among us report dreams that are vivid and bizarre. Currently, there is an argument in psychology based on conflicting data showing that creative people dream differently – either having shorter, more intense dreams or longer, more involved dreams.

ARE YOU HAPPY?

People need not be dark and depressed to be creative. Three researchers from the University of Maryland made people happy by either giving them a bag of sweets or letting them watch a short comedy film. A 'neutral' group watched a maths movie while a 'negative' group had to sit through a brief Nazi documentary. You guessed it: the happy people performed better on creativity tests.

Why does happiness lead to creativity? The researchers suggest that the brains of happy people more readily access existing knowledge. The more knowledge there is available, the easier it is to put different concepts together and form original thoughts. These psychologists used the wordsmith's test – a quiz thought to measure how well we can mesh different concepts.

Now here is something else that's interesting: creativity can *cause* happiness. An article in the *Journal of Creative Behavior* postulates that creative people are happier because they come up with more good ideas than average people. If happiness can be spoiled by unsolved problems, and creative people have fewer unsolved problems, then they should be happier. For more information on the benefits of happiness, see chapter 5.

WERE YOU THE CLASS CLOWN?

There are many studies that show that humour requires creativity, but here is a little twist. It turns out that children up to the age of fifteen do not need to be creative to be funny. However, beyond this age humour is definitely linked to creativity. Why? It seems that children are an easy audience. A class clown only needs to shout out 'knickers' to make the audience howl with appreciation. However, as we move into late adolescence and adulthood, humour requires more wit and creativity. Incidentally, there is a higher correlation of creativity and humour in women than in men. I imagine that's why some men still try to get away with the old 'knickers' gag.

DO YOU DRINK FOR INSPIRATION?

There is a popular notion that drinking alcohol stimulates creativity. Well, according to Geoff Lowe of the University of Hull, it's untrue.

He found that when people have a few drinks their creativity remains unchanged. It may even go down a little.

William Lapp and his colleagues from the Research Institute on Addictions found the same effect; however, unlike the previous experiment, their drinks were served with a twist. The experimenters fooled some people into *thinking* they were drinking alcohol when they only got tonic water. It turns out that while drinking has no impact on creativity, the *idea* that you have been drinking does! Students who were tricked into thinking they had been boozing produced significantly more creative works. So while alcohol may make you think you're great, you'll be more creative without it.

ARE YOU RAISING CREATIVE KIDS?

Children are wonderfully creative individuals. Their thirst for knowledge and ignorance of rules makes for fantastic originality. Psychologist Teresa Amabile found that you can foster your child's creativity by allowing them to play in an atmosphere void of these five creativity killers:

Creativity Killers

Surveillance: Don't always look over their shoulders. Give children the opportunity to create in a caring environment that is less structured and supervised. It is hard to be creative when someone is always watching you.

Judgement: Children should judge their own work. Adult criticism can come across as harsh. Children should create for their personal satisfaction rather than for their parents' acceptance.

Competition: Children should not be put in a win/lose situation where only the 'best' gets the prize. It is extremely difficult to judge the creativity of many works. Often art varies so widely that there is never one best entry. Children will have plenty of opportunity to be exposed to competition in other aspects of life.

Rules: Don't tell kids exactly how they should do things. For children to become creative adults, we must encourage them to find better ways to do things on their own. Rigid adherence to rules is a creativity killer.

Pressure: Expectations are good; pressure to perform is bad. Creativity comes best when it arises internally from the child. Parents can snuff out the internal drive to create by applying unrealistic pressure.

CAN YOU TAP INTO YOUR INGENUITY?

So, you're at work and you have to write a project, make a presentation, or you have a problem but you don't know where to begin or what to include. You need a dose of creativity. But how can you get it? Try *mind mapping*. Mind mapping is a visual, nonlinear way to organise information. All you need is a pencil and paper and you can creatively mind map. To tap your creative reservoir, do this:

- Take a blank piece of paper and write a word that represents the task at hand. This could be a problem, an agenda, or any dilemma you face.

- Think about that word for sixty seconds.

- Write every conceivable word that is related to the problem and its solutions around the edges of the paper. Do not censor your ideas. Allow your mind to run free. Keep writing until the task word is surrounded by your thoughts.

- Draw a line from each word to the problem. Then, on each line, write how you get from the problem to the solution. If you generate several similar ideas, hook your lines together like the branch of a tree.

- If appropriate, ask colleagues to help brainstorm. Post the mind-mapping sheet on the wall and let others contribute. Often ideas from other departments can be extremely useful.

- You can use colours or symbols to organise your thoughts. Soon you will have a 'thought picture'. Use these ideas and your organisation to address the problem. Periodically revisit the mind map to come up with fresh ideas.

Before you know it you will have outlined solutions and organised your thoughts. Mind mapping is so easy and fun to do that the only real challenge is to start.

WANT TO INCREASE YOUR CREATIVITY?

It's easy – if you're a woman. All you have to do is ovulate. Science has proved that women who are about to ovulate have increased levels of creativity, do more divergent thinking and generate more new ideas. Isn't the body wonderful? During this stage of the menstrual cycle women also tend to be a little more jealous, but they cope with it better. They are less aggressive and more constructive when problem solving.

WANT TO IMPROVE YOUR CREATIVITY?
TRY THESE TECHNIQUES

- *Vary your routine:* Do something a little different every day; keep your brain guessing. Go to work along a different route; eat something different; talk to a stranger.

- *Study something in detail:* Look at a postage stamp under a magnifying glass; stare at a flower until your eyes cross; memorise a poem.

- *Exercise your mind:* Pretend you need to hammer a nail and you don't have either; calculate how much something weighs without a scale. Stretch your creative muscles by looking at everyday items in a new context.

- *Fantasize:* Pretend you have a doorway in your home that leads to anywhere in time or space. By passing through the door, you could encounter Darth Vader, have dinner with a group of Neanderthals, or ride on an electron as it zips around a proton.

- *Reflect:* Don't always *do,* sometimes just *be.*

- *Lose track of time:* Become completely absorbed in your task; do not watch the clock; ignore your surroundings and become at one with the matter at hand.

- *Think in opposites:* Imagine a world where chocolate has no calories, all children are well mannered and men are sensitive.

- *Learn:* Go to the library or a museum.

- *Be invisible:* Imagine what you would do if you were invisible for a day. If you could go anywhere undetected, where would it be, what would you do and who would you see?

- *Keep a notebook:* Jot down ideas, no matter how ridiculous they might seem; if you drive a lot, use a mini recorder.

- *Write a journal:* not filled with the present, but with stories of your life for dates a month from now, next year, five years from today, etc.

- *Network:* Find others who share your interests; search the Internet or find a club; bounce your ideas off someone in your field. Have a good laugh with friends.

- *Take a class:* Study something that interests you.

- *Research:* Learn more about your favourite activity.

- *Take a nap:* Give yourself some downtime; let your mind wander.

- *Relax:* Spend an extra two minutes parked in your car whenever you go somewhere. Use this time for peaceful, relaxing thought.

- *Play:* Pick up the sport you lost the time for; tinker on a musical instrument; throw a Frisbee or go for a hike.

3

RELATIONSHIPS

To the world you are just one person,
but to one person you are the world. UNKNOWN

Relationships! Psychology bit off more than it could chew trying to analyse something as complex as human relationships. But, you don't have to go to school to study this subject. We are all experts in our own way. We are all intimately involved in relationships from birth. We depend on our mothers and fathers, fight with our brothers and sisters, make friends and fall in love. No one can live completely alone.

Whether casually or intimately, we need the company of others. The support of a friend, family member or lover who shares our attitudes increases our feelings of self-worth. Without them life would be boring and meaningless, like that of a prisoner sentenced

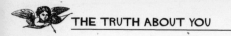

to solitary confinement. Most animals, when isolated, suffer severe stress – they pace, tear at their fur and feathers, and become listless. Under the same circumstances, wouldn't you?

So how do we form relationships? In public, we exchange casual greetings with acquaintances as well as strangers, making others feel comfortable. These brief interactions make our daily routines more interesting and fulfilling. With friends we form deeper bonds by lending emotional support, sharing opinions and drawing on common experiences. It takes skill to build a good relationship, and those who lack the know-how end up lonely. Especially when it comes to romance.

LEARNING RELATIONSHIP SKILLS TAKES A LIFETIME!

As babies, we are clueless when it comes to forming a relationship. We soil ourselves, express the slightest discomfort by screaming and crying, and are utterly helpless. We repay our parents' constant care and daily attention by keeping them up all night and bellowing for more. A mother may sacrifice career, sleep and leisure to attend to a family member who cannot walk, speak or perform any useful function. Exhausted, she will slave, scrub, cradle and coo with undivided attention – and what might a baby do to make such constant sacrifice seem worthwhile? Smile.

Soon, however, a child's interaction goes far beyond facial expression. Children learn to contribute, making their relationships less one-sided. They learn the roles of parent and child, boys and girls. Though still utterly dependent, they are able to help with tasks, pick up their toys and assume other small responsibilities. They develop conversation skills and can show more affection. As their personalities become more complex, kids form stronger and more interesting bonds with others. Beyond the world of mum, dad and siblings, there is a desire to play with friends. These friendships, however, are at first based more on toys and possessions than personal interdependence. The immediate family is still the centre of social life.

It isn't until early adolescence that most children begin to search for their own identity and break from the family unit. In an effort to become independent, young people look to their friends for companionship and answers, and suddenly, taking part in family activities is embarrassing. However, because they are still dependent on their parents for resources and are still developing emotionally, freedom comes awkwardly. As teens, they look towards friends for emotional support and may share a generational subculture foreign to adults. Language, clothes and hairstyles can become the basis for friendships. Emotions are raw and transparent, and relationships can be both intense and volatile. Newfound sexuality brings forth frenetic energy and insecurity. When it comes to rela-tionships, adolescence is a time for experimenting and testing boundaries; it is a time for sampling. Most agree that it is a good stage to grow out of.

By the time we reach adulthood, we are supposed to know who we are. We have dated, experimented with friendship and romance, and developed a well-rounded personality. Many now feel the pressure to form the relationship that will last a lifetime. Sharing a physically and emotionally intimate relationship with another adult is traditionally the final step in our fulfilment as individuals. It is also crucial to the kind of legacy we will leave, as a long-term union often includes the raising of children. Finding the right person is a tall order.

Romantic love may be characterised by obsessiveness, idealism and sexual arousal. Symptoms include increased heart rate, inability to concentrate, sleeplessness, sweating and weakness – no wonder they call it *lovesickness*. At any rate, these feelings cannot be sustained indefinitely and are hardly the foundation for a life-long relationship. As a result, romance is often the basis for beginning a partnership, but is seldom what allows it to endure. Luckily, love also includes intimacy and commitment. These are the aspects that keep relationships grounded long after passion has waned. In the best relationships, romance is constantly being redis-covered as commitment and intimacy grow deeper and couples share life's surprises.

Those who form lasting relationships are likely to be happy in old age. With the pressures of child rearing behind them and the comfort of a life partner and old friends, their honed relationship skills have paid off. Old loves have become deep friendships. It is a time to enjoy.

A BRIEF HISTORY OF RELATIONSHIP TESTING: HOW WE GOT HERE

Psychology has long been intrigued with the study of romantic relationships. Several tests of marital success were devised in the 1920s and 1930s. These early tests sought to measure happiness in traditional marriages. But times change. In the 1950s, a new set of relationship tests was developed to remain up to date with the changing roles of romantic relationships. The redefining of sex roles in the 1960s and 1970s caused yet another wave of updated relationship tests. The old wording and concepts seemed out of date. The late 1980s and early 1990s also saw a greater acceptance of cohabiting and gay and lesbian couples.

In the late 1980s, a Texas psychologist, Susan Hendrick, saw the need for a short but accurate test that would be easy to take. This test was created partially in response to the need to assess nontraditional couples. It is appropriate for many kinds of couples, including those who are married, gay, living together, and just dating. It is also an excellent tool for predicting whether couples will stay together. Dr Hendrick has brought relationship testing into modern times with this wonderful, yet thought-provoking, little test.

At the same time Susan Hendrick developed the relationship satisfaction quiz, three psychologists from Minnesota and Kansas developed a test of relationship *strength*. Ellen Berscheid and her colleagues were interested in what couples do together and how they influence each other. We will start with relationship satisfaction and then move on to its strength.

TAKING THE RELATIONSHIP SATISFACTION TEST

This test is easy to take because there are only seven questions. But don't be fooled; these are seven important questions. Give each one some thought. Do not rush. As you answer the questions think about your relationship with your partner. There are no right or wrong answers. Because so much of the fun in this test is comparing your answers to your partner's, be sure to share it with your loved one.

TEST YOURSELF

INSTRUCTIONS
This questionnaire focuses on your relationship with your partner. Take this test at a time when you are comfortable and

not distracted. It takes about ten minutes to complete, but there is no time limit. When you are ready, the test starts below and you may begin. Mark your answers on the page by circling the number that best represents your opinion.

Do not rush through this test. Take your time. Carefully think about your relationship with your partner. Have fun!

HOW SATISFYING IS YOUR RELATIONSHIP?

Indicate below the number that best answers each of the following questions for you:

1. How well does your partner meet your needs?

Poorly		Average		Extremely Well
1	2	3	4	5

2. In general, how satisfied are you with your relationship?

Dissatisfied		Average		Extremely Satisfied
1	2	3	4	5

3. How good is your relationship compared to most?

Poor		Average		Excellent
1	2	3	4	5

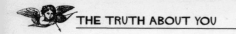
4. How often do you wish you hadn't got into this relationship?

Never		Average		Very Often
1	2	3	4	5

5. To what extent has your relationship met your original expectations?

Hardly at All		Average		Completely
1	2	3	4	5

6. How much do you love your partner?

Not Much		Average		Very Much
1	2	3	4	5

7. How many problems are there in your relationship?

Very Few		Average		Very Many
1	2	3	4	5

END OF TEST   **Your Score:** _____

Susan Hendrick, 'A Generic Measure of Relationship Satisfaction',
Journal of Marriage and Family, 1988, 50, 93–98. Used by permission.

Scoring Your Test

Scoring this test is simple. Add the seven numbers you circled and write your score on the bottom of the test page. Notice that the scoring for questions 4 and 7 are reversed. It is supposed to be that way.

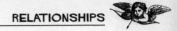
Understanding Your Score

This test has been given to so many people that we can convert your score into a percentile. However, there may be a danger in reading too much into your percentile on this test, because most of the people tested to derive the percentiles were college students who reported being 'in love'. Because college students tend to be in the earlier, more romantic phases of their relationships, you may find your score to be a little lower than expected. If you are in a long-term relationship, you will find it more informative to compare your answers to your partner's.

YOUR SCORE	PERCENTILE	CONCLUSION
23	15th	*Dissatisfied*
26	30th	*Ho-Hum*
29	50th	*Pleased*
32	60th	*Delighted*
35	85th	*Enchanted*

What Does Your Score Mean?

What does it mean to have a score of 20, or 30, or 40? I wish it could say that you are a wonderful person in a glorious relationship, and

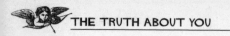

you will live happily ever after. However, tests have not become quite that accurate yet.

Of the college students on whom this test was standardised, the average relationship score was 29. Forty per cent of the people who took this test scored between 26 and 32. That is a fairly tight range.

YOUR SCORE
Score of 7–25. Not Cinderella!
Your relationship is no Cinderella story. You are dissatisfied with your current prince/princess. Your score indicates that 70 per cent or more of the population are happier in their relationships than you are. Perhaps a recent argument might have lowered your total a little, but your score indicates that your relationship has problems. You may believe that the passion has gone out of your relationship, that your partner is playing games with you or that you are simply tired of doing all the giving. If you have invested a great deal of time into your relationship and wish to continue with this person, you must focus on building consensus and cohesion where possible. Now is the time to have a long, hard look at your relationship and discuss your needs and expectations. I encourage you and your partner to take the sexual attitudes and happiness tests in chapters 4 and 5 and see the end of this chapter for further suggestions. It will take some work, but maybe you can turn your romance into a fairy tale.

Score of 26–32. Happily Ever After!

Your relationship is about as charmed as most couples'. You and your partner probably have the ordinary ups and downs that many couples do, but in general, you are quite satisfied. There is, however, room for improvement. Review your scores together for clues on which areas need enhancement. For example, if one of you believes that your relationship has not met original expectations, talk about what your expectations are. Your partner would probably be happy to fulfil them. Maybe you just have not made your needs clear. Also, many differences are a matter of perspective. Perhaps your loved one does something that drives you mad but does not realise it or see it as a problem. Get these issues out in the open so you can both review them.

Finally, be sure that you both complete the tests in the chapters 'Sex and Desire' and 'Happiness'. Compare and discuss your results on those tests too, then see the end of each chapter for suggestions for improvement.

Score of 33–35. Fairy Tales Do Come True!

You are exceptionally satisfied in your relationship. You are probably happier than 70 per cent of couples. Congratulations on having built a gratifying partnership. You and your partner respect and love each other tremendously. You are also faithful to each other and honour each other's needs. You probably make love passionately. These are all essential ingredients for a blissful relationship. If

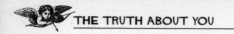

you have children, they are getting a good foundation to build their future partnerships.

However, be careful about becoming complacent. You have something wonderful, so do not take it for granted. You probably know that it is hard work keeping a relationship healthy – although it is a labour of love, it still requires hard work. If you have been with your partner for many years, it may take effort to keep the passion alive. You must identify your weaknesses and shore them up. For example, if you tend to be self-centred, you must remind yourself to be more giving. But given the wonderful score you obtained, you are in exceptional shape for a long and happy relationship.

How Strong Is Your Relationship?

TAKING THE TEST

Now that we know how satisfied you are with your relationship, let's see how *strong* it is. This next quiz will help you think about your relationship in different ways. For example, you may be in a wonderfully caring situation, but it may be fleeting. Or maybe you long for a little more pizzazz, but you have a rock-steady partner. These thirty-four questions permit you to measure the potency of your bonds by determining how much your partner influences your innermost thoughts, feelings and goals.

TEST YOURSELF

INSTRUCTIONS

This questionnaire focuses on the strength of your relationship with your partner by asking questions about how you are influenced by your loved one. Take this test at a time when you are comfortable and not distracted. It takes about ten to fifteen minutes to complete, but there is no time limit. When you are ready, you may begin. Mark your answers on the page by circling the number that best represents your opinion.

Take your time. Think carefully think about your relationship with your partner. Answer each question honestly and have fun!

HOW STRONG IS YOUR RELATIONSHIP?

Indicate below the extent to which you agree or disagree with each of the following:

YOUR PARTNER'S INFLUENCES ON YOUR FEELINGS AND BEHAVIOUR

1. My partner will influence my future financial security.

Strongly Disagree						Strongly Agree
1	2	3	4	5	6	7

2. My partner does not influence everyday things in my life.

Strongly Disagree   Strongly Agree

7   6   5   4   3   2   1

3. My partner influences important things in my life.

1   2   3   4   5   6   7

4. My partner influences which parties and other social events I attend.

1   2   3   4   5   6   7

5. My partner influences the extent to which I accept responsibilities in our relationship.

1   2   3   4   5   6   7

6. My partner does not influence how much time I spend doing household work.

7   6   5   4   3   2   1

7. My partner does not influence how I choose to spend my money.

7   6   5   4   3   2   1

8. My partner influences the way I feel about myself.

1   2   3   4   5   6   7

9. My partner does not influence my moods.

Strongly Disagree						Strongly Agree
7	6	5	4	3	2	1

10. My partner influences the basic values that I hold.

1	2	3	4	5	6	7

11. My partner does not influence the opinions that I have of other important people in my life.

7	6	5	4	3	2	1

12. My partner does not influence when I see, and the amount of time I spend with, my family.

7	6	5	4	3	2	1

13. My partner influences when I see, and the amount of time I spend with, friends.

1	2	3	4	5	6	7

14. My partner does not influence which of my friends I see.

7	6	5	4	3	2	1

15. My partner does not influence the type of career I have.

7	6	5	4	3	2	1

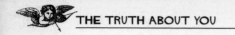

16. My partner influences or will influence how much time I devote to my career.

Strongly Disagree   Strongly Agree

1   2   3   4   5   6   7

17. My partner does not influence my chances of getting a good job in the future.

7   6   5   4   3   2   1

18. My partner influences the way I feel about the future.

7   6   5   4   3   2   1

19. My partner does not have the capacity to influence how I act in various situations.

7   6   5   4   3   2   1

20. My partner influences and contributes to my overall happiness.

1   2   3   4   5   6   7

21. My partner does not influence my present financial security.

7   6   5   4   3   2   1

22. My partner influences how I spend my free time.

1   2   3   4   5   6   7

23. My partner influences when I see him/her and the amount of time we spend together.

Strongly Disagree						Strongly Agree
1	2	3	4	5	6	7

24. My partner does not influence how I dress.

7	6	5	4	3	2	1

25. My partner influences how I decorate my home.

1	2	3	4	5	6	7

26. My partner does not influence where I live.

7	6	5	4	3	2	1

27. My partner influences what I watch on TV.

1	2	3	4	5	6	7

YOUR PARTNER'S INFLUENCES ON YOUR GOALS AND PLANS

For these final questions, circle the number that indicates how much your partner affects your plans and goals. If a statement does not apply to you, circle a 1.

1. My vacation plans.

Not at All						To a Great Extent
1	2	3	4	5	6	7

2. My marriage plans.*

Not at All						To a Great Extent
1	2	3	4	5	6	7

3. My plans to have children.

1	2	3	4	5	6	7

4. My plans to make major investments.

1	2	3	4	5	6	7

5. My plans to join a club, social organisation, church, etc.

1	2	3	4	5	6	7

6. My school- or job-related plans.

1	2	3	4	5	6	7

7. My plans for achieving a particular standard of living.*

1	2	3	4	5	6	7

* If you are married, indicate 7.

END OF TEST

Ellen Berscheid, Mark Snyder and Allen M. Omoto, 'Relationship Closeness Inventory',
Journal of Personality and Social Psychology, 1989, 57, 729–807. Used by permission.

Scoring Your Test

Scoring this test is as simple as 1, 2, 3:

1. Add the numbers you circled for the first twenty-seven questions on your partner's influences of your feelings and behaviour and write that number here: _____

2. Add the seven numbers you circled in the goals and plans section and write that number here: _____

3. Add both scores together here: _____

> *Notice that some of the numbers for scoring*
> *are deliberately reversed.*

Understanding Your Score

This quiz is actually part of a larger test given to hundreds of romantic partners. I have calculated percentiles for you below, but please remember, like many psychological tests, the figures are based on college students. If you are in a long-term relationship, you will find it more informative to compare your answers to your partner's.

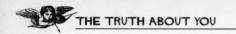

YOUR SCORE	PERCENTILE	CONCLUSION
93 and lower	15th	*Feeble*
94 to 113	30th	*Delicate*
114 to 133	50th	*Firm*
134 to 153	70th	*Robust*
154 and higher	85th	*Potent*

WHAT DOES YOUR SCORE MEAN?

This test gives you a measure of the strength of your relationship. It is best used in conjunction with the relationship satisfaction test. If you have a satisfying and strong bond with your partner, that is great. But there are other outcomes. The table below shows how the results of both tests can be compared. Choose your strength result from the columns and your satisfaction outcome from the rows.

		STRENGTH	
		Weaker	**Stronger**
SATISFACTION	**Less Happy**	Time to Move On?	You Have Work to Do.
	More Happy	A Fleeting Romance?	Rock Solid. Good for You!

YOUR SCORE

The strength of a relationship is like the ties that bind two people together. We can enjoy the company of another, but are we coupled to that person?

Score of 113 or Lower. Thin Thread.

The ties that bind you are weak. You are held together by wisps of thread. Although it may appear pretty, it is hard to sustain a relationship with so slight a bond. However, if you are in a budding romance, your strength will grow. While brown paper packages tied up with strings may be a few of your favourite things, you will need more than this to nurture your flings.

But all is not lost. This could be good news if you are not satisfied with your partner, but clearly bad news if you want to be well tied to that someone special. If you want to tie up your favourite mate for life, review the relationship exercises at the end of the chapter for strengthening pointers.

Score of 114 to 133. Bungee Cords.

You have a healthy and strong relationship, but it grows slack at times as if lashed together with bungee cords. Your closeness wavers with elasticity and the distance between you fluctuates. This is quite average for most relationships; however, nearly everyone in this group would prefer stronger bonds with someone special.

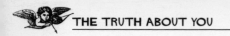

Score of 134 Or higher. Steel Cables.

Your relationship is as strong as steel cables – you could support a suspension bridge with your attachment! Other couples should bow before you and your partner and learn from your love and skills. You and your mate are either exceptionally communicative and open, or long-term lovers whose lives are entwined in an intricate pattern of support for each other.

IF YOUR SCORE WAS NOT AS HIGH AS YOU WANTED

Relationships with loved ones are a tremendously important part of life. Most of us long for a higher score than we get on these tests. If you anticipated a better score than you got, talk to your partner about the following issues and make sure you make your expectations and desires crystal clear. Then, carefully listen (without interruption) to your partner's views.

DISCUSS THESE TOPICS TO IMPROVE YOUR RELATIONSHIP:

- Do you respect me?
- Will you always be faithful?

- What can I do to make sex better for you?
- Can we agree on how to spend our money?
- What are the important aspects of raising children?
- Are you pleased with the way chores are shared at home?
- Can we work together on personal projects that interest us both?

How Do You Compare?

Now that you have measured your relationship, let's look at the psychology of love and see how you compare to others who have taken relationship tests.

HOW DO I LOVE THEE? LET ME COUNT THE WAYS.

According to the scientific journals, there are five ways to experience love. These types of love are not mutually exclusive, but we do tend to move between them as our relationships grow. The five stages of love are:

1. **Intuitive Love.** This is the mesmerising, hot looks and wonderful sex kind of love. This type of love involves much touching, gazing into each other's eyes and sexual adventure.
2. **Companionate Love.** This is the type of love that turns you and me into 'we'. This is the warm, gooey feeling of connectedness and sharing. There are no longer two individuals, but one couple.

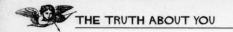

3. **Traditional Love.** We all remember this one. It is the puppy love of youth; the love that creates anxiousness and anticipation; the love that makes you so lovesick, you lose your appetite.

4. **Secure Love.** For some people, love is a warm security blanket used to protect themselves from a cold world. This kind of love makes you feel wanted, needed and complete.

5. **Committed Love.** This is the serious stuff. It is the kind of love that makes you plan for the future, discuss weddings, children and old age together. If you are bitten by this love bug, you are ready to commit your life to your 'other half'.

ARE YOU ADDICTED TO LOVE?

If you have ever fallen head-over-heels in love, you know that your mind abandons your senses and hormones preclude rational thought. During this time, a little molecule called *phenylethylamine* (we'll call it PEA) drives your body to do the wildest, most foolhardy things. PEA is like an amphetamine: It makes you excited, euphoric and energised. With a little PEA, you can make conversation all evening and love all night. This is the drug that turns some of us into love junkies. Some get addicted to the intense stimulant properties of PEA and seek out romantic relationships to satisfy their craving by repeatedly falling for someone new. You see, to manufacture PEA the body needs an experience that is new and exciting. The same partner just doesn't excite the body the way a new one does.

For most of us, the production of PEA decreases within a few weeks, and we begin to see our partner more clearly. It is at this point that we either begin a lasting relationship built on personality traits, or we take a hard look at the loser lying next to us in bed and wonder what we ever saw in the louse.

The body also uses PEA to alert us of problems other than falling in love. PEA is released into the blood stream in times of danger, novelty, stress and fear. The problem is that our brains are easily fooled by our heart's little helper. As a result, people are much more likely to fall in love in novel or dangerous circumstances; hence all the fervour of holiday and wartime romances.

WOULD YOU CLIMB THE HIGHEST MOUNTAIN AND SWIM THE DEEPEST SEA?

Donald Dutton and Arthur Aron from British Columbia designed a beautiful experiment that demonstrates the power of PEA – Cupid's love juice. In a nutshell, they interviewed men as they crossed a bridge. Half of the men were tested on a precarious, 450-foot long wooden suspension bridge with a wire handrail. (You can imagine the rush these guys felt as they crossed a swaying, bouncing bridge hanging over a 200-foot drop into a rocky ravine below.) The fellows met a young woman interviewer halfway across. In the midst of the swaying and the rolling, the interviewer asked each man individually to fill out a brief questionnaire and write a short story. When he was done, she tore off a corner of paper, wrote her

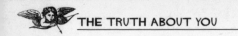

name and phone number, and gave it to the unsuspecting subject in case he was 'interested in more information about the study'.

Of course, no experiment is complete without a control group. Other men were out walking over a big, sturdy bridge anchored over a brook ten feet below, where they met the same young woman who gave them the same procedure. Then, all the experimenters had to do was count how many men from each group called the interviewer.

Naturally, the men who met the woman on the dangerous, wobbly bridge were calling her up and asking her out left and right, while the men who met her on the safe bridge just went on with life. Why? Because walking across the suspension bridge made them produce the molecule PEA like Niagara Falls. And so, the moral of the story is: either be careful where you fall in love (to be sure it really is love) or, if you are desperate for a date, hang around on dangerous bridges!

Music has charms to soothe a savage breast, to soften rocks, or bend a knotted oak. WILLIAM CONGREVE

CAN MUSIC HELP YOU FALL IN LOVE?

Trying to snag that winsome person you have been yearning for? Let a little music help. Deborah Blood and Stephen Ferriss put fifty pairs of strangers together in rooms and asked them to play a game. As each pair of potential lovers was getting to know each other, the experimenters played a little background music to some while others heard nothing. The results: background music makes for much more satisfying conversations. So apply this knowledge: next time you are with that special someone play some cheery Chopin, Haydn or Liszt quietly in the background. You will be perceived as a stunning conversationalist and a good catch.

IS YOUR DATE MORE ATTRACTIVE AT THE END OF THE EVENING?

And speaking of classical music, there is an old country song that includes the lyrics 'Don't the girls all get prettier at closing time?' Well, several University of Virginia psychologists thought that theory was worth a closer look. The song even suggested how to conduct the study: it went on to say, 'If I could rate them on a scale of one to ten . . . looking for a nine but an eight could fit right in.' To test this hypothesis, the researchers went to several bars one evening and asked patrons to rate the attractiveness of the other customers. Sure enough, both men and women found their potential dates to be more attractive as the night wore on. Why does this happen?

The answer is in the rest of the song: 'Ain't it funny, ain't it strange, the way a man's opinions change, when he starts to face that lonely night.' It seems that as your dating options dwindle, you settle and become more satisfied with your options. This makes you reassess the situation and causes each possible mate to look more attractive.

IS YOUR MAN BALD?

Men and hair, hair and men. What is more crushing to a man's sexuality than losing his hair? This is not a new problem for guys. The oldest medical prescription to stop baldness dates back to the Egyptians, five thousand years ago. We know that as men lose their hair, their testosterone drops and they become less aggressive.

Are women subconsciously attracted to hairless men because they remind women of babies – all big bald heads and eyes? Do these baby-like features stimulate maternal instincts? A couple of psychologists sought to learn just what people think of the personalities of bald men. To make life a little more interesting, they also threw beards into their experiment. College students were given photographs of men made up to look bald, full haired, bearded or clean shaven. The results are fascinating:

RESULTS OF BALD/BEARD RESEARCH

	Bald	Haired
Bearded	Unattractive	Dangerous
	Poor lover	Dominant
	Impotent	Less educated
	Brave	Dishonest
	Experienced	Likely to have an affair
Clean shaven	Intelligent	Handsome
	Educated	Desirable dating partner
	Honest	Good lover
	Helpful	Potent
	Faithful	Affectionate

What is going on here? It is thought that perhaps baldness evolved in men as a signal. A shining head from a distance would indicate to a stranger that the bald man was not aggressive and threatening, but someone with knowledge of resources like food, shelter and water.

WOULD YOU DATE SOMEONE OF ANOTHER RACE?

More than half of Americans asked this question replied 'yes'. According to a national study of two thousand Americans conducted for the *Washington Post,* America is slowly becoming a more tolerant nation. Two out of three people under thirty-five would date someone of a different race if they were single, yet only one in three people over fifty answered the same. Americans are less liberal when the topic moves from dating to marriage. White women are the least likely to marry a man outside of their race. Only about one-third of white women would consider an interracial marriage. On the other hand, African American men are most tolerant; over two-thirds would consider marrying a woman of another race.

CAN EXERCISE HELP YOU LAND A MATE?

The answer is 'yes', but don't worry, you don't even have to sweat. The expression 'no pain, no gain' does not apply here – if you know about *excitation transfer*. When it comes to using this fascinating principle, timing is everything.

It is common knowledge that when we exercise, our heart beats wildly, our skin flushes and we sweat. Some even feel a mild sense

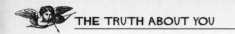

of euphoria. These physical responses are expected; our bodies know what is going on. But after a good workout, it takes a while for our bodies to return to normal. During this lag time, our heart rate remains high, we continue to perspire and we have a healthy radiance. This is the time to bump into someone you would like to meet. Provided you wait until your potential mate has finished exercising, their unsuspecting body may misread its warm and fuzzy glow. It thinks: 'My heart is all atwitter, I'm all hot and steamy, I must be in love!' People regularly transfer their excited states incorrectly. To apply this knowledge and catch a mate, hang out outside of health clubs, tennis courts, swimming pools, etc.

HAVE YOU SEEN THE GREEN-EYED MONSTER?

Jealousy is an alarm system that tells you when an intruder has invaded an important relationship. But it can quickly change loving into loathing; especially when the alarm repeatedly goes off without cause. What makes you most jealous? Let's tease your imagination for a moment:

JEALOUSY QUIZ

Imagine these two scenarios:

1. Close your eyes and imagine your partner is enjoying wild, passionate sexual intercourse with another good-looking, healthy

individual. They are trying all sorts of sexual positions and having mind-blowing orgasms.

Okay, calm down for a minute.

2. Now close your eyes and imagine your partner falling in love with someone else. Your partner comes to you and tells you he/she loves another and no longer loves you.

Which scenario makes you most upset?

While neither scenario is appealing, the chances are if you are a man, the thought of your partner having sex with another drives you nuts. Conversely, if you are a woman, the idea that your partner would fall in love with another is maddening. Incidentally, there is evidence to suggest that the more happily married men are, the more outraged they become with the notion of spousal infidelity.

These sex differences are cross-cultural and have been demonstrated in countries including the Netherlands, Germany and the United States. But why are we wired this way? We need to go back to our evolutionary roots for answers. For primitive man, a mate's sexual infidelity was a catastrophe. He may have been duped into spending his life providing for and raising another man's child. If he did not pass his genes to the next generation, he was a genetic failure. It would have been okay for early man if his wife loved another man as long as she bore and cared for his children.

Primitive women, on the other hand, needed to be assured that they would always have their protector and provider looking out for them. If her man was smitten with another woman, she might have lost him and the resources he provided, and that might mean the end of her genetic lineage. It would have been tolerable for her if her man impregnated other women, as long as he provided for her.

It may not be romance, but it is our history.

ARE MEN RULED BY THEIR GENES?

In case you are a little sceptical about the idea that our relationship behaviours are linked to our ancestry, have a look at this wonderful study.

Dr Tony Goldberg, a Harvard University anthropologist, counted the number of people who gave money to beggars. Throughout the summer of 1992 he observed almost sixty-four hundred people pass by male and female beggars who were alone and with no obvious physical or mental disabilities. Dr Goldberg found some interesting things, such as, only about 2 per cent of people who passed by made a donation and that on busy streets beggars could earn between $1.25 and $30.00 an hour. But the fascinating thing he found was that significantly more men gave money to female beggars – but only when the men were walking alone. If a man was with a woman, he would ignore the female beggar. This was not the case with male beggars. Regardless of whether a male passerby was alone or with a woman, the male beggar had the same chance of getting a donation.

What does this behaviour mean? Giving to beggars is not an entirely selfless act. Although the men presumably had no interest in forming relationships with the female beggars, they are wired to bond with women but, of course, not in the presence of their mates. When men think nobody is watching they let their wandering genes express themselves.

DO YOU WEAR PERFUME?

Many women believe that sophisticated clothing and the sensuous smell of their favourite perfume will help them attract a man. Be careful. Too much of a good thing can put off potential mates. Some Purdue researchers ran an experiment in which almost one hundred college-aged men worked briefly with women who were dressed either formally with a neat blouse and skirt, or informally in jeans and a sweatshirt. The women also either wore perfume or remained unscented. After working with the women for a few minutes, the experimenter asked them how attractive they thought their work partner was.

Now here is the rub. There were only two women; they took turns dressing up or down and wearing the perfume or not. The result? A dab of perfume on a girl in jeans is a real turn-on for young bucks, but women who wear perfume when they are dressed

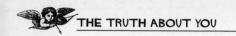

up can be a turnoff. Why? It seems that women in fancy clothes and perfume are seen by men as aloof and unattainable. Incidentally, the casual jeans look and no perfume was not a big hit with most guys. The men considered neatly dressed women as both more attractive and more likeable.

DID YOU EVER WANT TO DATE A LIVING BARBIE DOLL?

Barbie is, without question, the most popular doll ever invented. Some one billion (yes, that is 1,000,000,000) Barbies have been sold worldwide. But what about her sexy shape?

What about those fellows who want to date a living Barbie doll? Well, they are pretty much out of luck. A group of Australian physical education professors calculated that the chances of meeting a human with the proportions of Barbie's physique are less than one hundred thousand to one. Ladies, your chances of meeting Ken incarnate are considerably better – about fifty to one.

DO YOU TRUST YOUR PARTNER?

And speaking of infidelity and jealousy, trust is a delicately fragile requirement in any relationship. It is a prerequisite for relationship success, yet it can be shattered easily.

How do you know when a man is lying?
You can see his lips moving. FORMER GIRLFRIEND

How do you know when someone is telling you the truth? When they look you straight in the eye? Not necessarily. When a man is lying to a woman, he is more likely to look into her eyes *longer*. Women do the same; when they lie they hold their gaze even longer. In fact, the only gender combination who can pull off an undetectable lie is two men talking to each other. The liar's eye contact will be no different from the honest fellow's.

CAN YOU HEAR A LIE?

However, there is more to lying than meets the eye. A British study asked one hundred thousand people to find a fib on TV, on the radio and in the newspaper. Almost three-quarters of them detected the lie on the radio, two-thirds found it in the newspaper, but only half caught it in the television broadcast. Why? People can control their body language much better than their voices when they deceive. So now you know: if you think someone is lying to you, just close your eyes and listen.

Incidentally, professional lie detectors such as police officers, judges and customs inspectors are no better at spotting a lie than the average college student. The professionals only think they are better detectors.

DO YOU LIE?

We all do it more than we would like to admit. While 90 per cent of us say it is hard to tell a lie, 20 per cent say they lie either occasionally

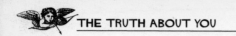

or frequently. Almost three-quarters of adults report they hardly ever lie, and one-quarter admit that lying is sometimes justified.

DO YOU SUFFER FROM FATAL ATTRACTION?

Diane Felmlee at the University of California studied 'Fatal Attraction', the condition in which the attribute you first find appealing eventually drives you up the wall. For example, you are attracted to someone who is always spontaneous and fun to be with. Later in the relationship, you discover your lover is just a fool who does not take your relationship seriously. About 20 per cent of people with fatal attractions report that they began a relationship with someone who was caring and considerate, only to later learn those qualities were really smothering jealously. A woman who is attracted to a powerful man may eventually be repelled by the same domineering attitude that first attracted her.

It may take a few months or many years for an attraction to become fatal. Also, when couples are dating they tend to be on their best behaviour. Often it is difficult to tell a mild eccentricity from a character flaw. The real intensity of your partner's attributes may not percolate to the surface until well into a long-term relationship.

Interestingly, people often use the same words to describe the initial attraction as the final rejection. The problems of fatal attraction are greatest in relationships where 'opposites attract'. They decrease when one is attracted to someone similar.

DO YOU LIKE TO SMOOCH?

How often should you kiss your spouse? Well, according to Chicago psychotherapist Sylvia Babbin, the average is four and a half times a day. Dr Babbin asked married people about their kissing habits while they were waiting for their planes at Chicago's O'Hare airport. This research includes all types of osculating from deep, passionate kisses to 'good-bye' pecks at the door. Why is kissing so important to humans? Kissing is extremely intimate; it brings us eye-to-eye and nose-to-nose. This is an intensely vulnerable position for us. It lowers our most basic psychological barriers and leaves us defenceless. Perhaps this is why prostitutes will engage in myriad sexual positions but many will not kiss their clients.

THE HEALTH BENEFITS OF KISSING

- Kissing requires trust. Biologically, we are cautious about anything getting too close to our eyes, nose and mouth. Kissing puts us in a delicate position and we must trust our partners.

- We have evolved the need to kiss to perform a little health check on our partner. While kissing we get close and look into their eyes, check out their skin and smell their breath. All indicators of health.

- Kissing is a great way to exercise. A kiss will burn two calories a minute – and if done right, it will lead to vigorous exercise.

- Brain candy – a good kiss releases endorphins in the brain and makes the body feel good.

- It's what the doctor ordered. Smooching bolsters your body's immune system and helps fight off germs.

DO YOU GET ENOUGH HUGS?

Kissing is great, but hugging may save your life. Dr Karen Grewen, a psychologist with the School of Medicine at the University of North Carolina, found that hugging and ten minutes of handholding with your partner greatly decreases the effects of stress. In her 2003 study, Dr Grewen tested two hundred couples: about half watched a pleasant video, held hands, then hugged for twenty seconds, and the other group rested alone. She then asked participants to describe a recent situation where they became angry and stressed. Normally, reliving stressful circumstances taxes heart rate and blood pressure, but those who had contact with their loved ones were much more calm.

WILL YOUR RELATIONSHIP LAST?

For relationships to endure, they need basic elements. There are eight ingredients for the glue that bonds us together.

Eight Ingredients for a Successful Relationship

Attractiveness You do not have to be a model, but good hygiene, grooming and manners are essential.

Enthusiasm People want to live with someone who is interesting and jocular.

Affection You need to care for your partner both emotionally and physically.

Communication You have to talk to one another about the good and the bad.

Honesty When you talk, make it the truth. Your partner must trust you.

Intelligence All of us want some stimulating discussions from time to time.

Compatibility Your spouse should be your best friend.

Acceptance Do not try to change your loved one; open acceptance is necessary.

If you have these eight ingredients, you can look forward to a long and happy relationship. If you believe your relationship is running a little low on one or two of these qualities, talk with your partner about it. Address these problems early, before they grow out of control. Even if your relationships are running wonderfully, 'check the oil' and talk about these elements to make sure your partner's expectations are being met.

DO YOU WANT TO LIVE LONGER?

Get married. You know the old saying, 'Can't live with them, can't live without them'? Well, science has proven that if you live with

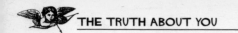

them, you will live longer. By examining information collected from eleven thousand Americans, researchers found plenty of evidence for the benefits of marriage. Why is marriage good for us? Two answers: married men live longer because they don't get to do the fun, crazy, life-threatening stuff they want to. Their cautious wives stop them from drinking, acting stupid and cutting their lives short. Married women live longer because they have someone bringing home the bacon, and they are better off financially than their single sisters. It seems that two can live as cheaply as one, and married couples accumulate more wealth, which, among other things, leads to better fitness and health care that, in turn, stretches out old age. Of course, emotional doting has to add a couple of years too. Kind of makes you feel sorry for those wild, fun-loving, free-spending, swinging singles, doesn't it?

HAVE YOU BEEN MARRIED A LONG TIME?

If you have been married for a long time, chances are you have grown to look like your spouse. How can that be? It seems that we tend to mimic our spouse's facial expressions. Day after day, as we age, we make the same smiles and sneers as our spouses, creating similar patterns of wrinkles around our eyes and mouths. Our faces actually grow to look like our lover's. But there is more: mimicking our loved ones over the years also brings us closer together. It turns out that older folks who look similar have happier marriages.

Want to Increase the Quality of Your Relationship?

- **Listen.** Become a good listener. Look people in the eye. Smile at them. Talk about the other person's interests, not your own. Show concern for others. We like people who like us and dislike people who dislike us.

- **Like.** Like yourself. Nobody is going to like you much if you don't like yourself. People with high self-esteem who take pride in their work are much more easy to like.

- **Be dependable.** People want someone whom they can rely on and trust.

- **Consider.** Measure your relationship. Ask yourself, how close does this person come to my ideal mate? If your partner does not match your imaginary perfect mate, do some soul-searching. Are your expectations unrealistic, or are you trying to bond with the wrong person?

- **Togetherness.** Spend time together, and spend it on fun things like conversation, playing and eating fine food. You can count the time spent together on chores, but only if you enjoy it.

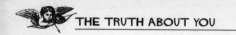

- **Romance.** Do romantic things together. No matter how long you have been together, it is important to weave some romance into your lives. What are these romantic things? A stroll along the beach, lying in front of a fire, going on a picnic, enjoying a quiet rowboat ride, a quiet dinner, a candlelit bath, or just simply enjoying an old movie late at night together.

4

SEX AND DESIRE

If I'm going to be a symbol of something, I'd rather have it sex.

MARILYN MONROE

Okay, how many of you skipped ahead to this chapter? If you did, don't be embarrassed. You are not the only one. Everyone is drawn to sex. Sex sells everything from books for your shelves to mud flaps for your tractor trailer. It is on radio, TV, billboards, books, newspapers and T-shirts. It influences us at home, work and play. Popular belief is that we all love sex and can't get enough. And when we aren't doing it, we are thinking about it. But is this true? And isn't sex supposed to be private?

First of all, we aren't doing it as much as you might think. The most sexed third of us copulates twice a week on average. Nothing to crow about. But three-quarters of us think about it daily. And as

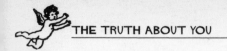

for its privacy, for a subject that is traditionally avoided in polite conversation, sex certainly has become public. While discussing your own bedroom exploits at a dinner party is considered boorish, the sex lives of public figures are prime conversational fodder. Private, yet public – why the paradox?

Perhaps the inherent privacy of the sexual act is what stimulates our curiosity. We know about our own unexceptional sex lives, but when it comes to the intimacies of anyone else, be it an alluring stranger at the other end of the phone line or a movie star glossing the cover of a tabloid, our curiosities are stirred. It brings out the Peeping Tom in us. We are titillated and respond with our imaginations and our wallets. The private becomes public, and people's deepest, most intimate feelings are churned into lame sitcoms and paper-thin advertising copy. Human bodies become objects, and magazines, movies and television crank out a barrage so thick that the average person is confronted with sex hundreds of times each day. Whether this is good or bad is for you to decide, but the existence of sex as a marketable commodity is undeniable.

WHY ARE WE SO INTERESTED IN SEX?

Has anyone ever told you that you are one of the sexiest primates on earth? Flattery will get me nowhere, you say? Well, it's true.

Your naked skin and nerve-filled nipples, lips, earlobes and breasts make you the perfect receiver for stroking, rubbing, pressing, kissing and caressing. If you are a male, your genitals are much larger than your hairy cousins', and if you are a female, you possess the rare capability of having sex daily, whether you are ovulating or not. As James Brown put it, you are 'like a sex machine'.

It all boils down to this: the reason we are so good at and so interested in having sex is so that we can form partnerships. Of course, continuing the species is important too; however, we could do that without so much as exchanging a kiss. In fact, with today's technology, we could do it without even touching. But our bodies yearn for sexual relations. We want to be held, kissed and have orgasms. And what better way than to have a constant, understanding partner who is devoted to fulfilling our needs.

Sexual pairing (as our biological friends call it) is the basis for human society. Two adults sharing the responsibilities of providing food, shelter and child care has allowed humanity to flourish, providing a safe, long-term environment for offspring and creating bonds that continue through generations. If it weren't for that sexual drive that tickles our interest from adolescence to infirmity, couples would be much less likely to stick together. And, as we have found in recent decades, broken families do not flourish nearly as well as those that are intact.

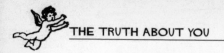

WHEN DO YOU HAVE SEX?

Chances are you are either a night person or a morning person, but the time of day is really not important. What is more important is the time of your life. Were you too young and irresponsible during your first sexual encounter, or did you lag behind your peers in finding an intimate physical relationship? Will your sex life peak before your partner's? And how long will your sex life last? Will it dwindle shortly after middle age, or will you be active till the day you die?

The good news is that most of us enjoy a long sex life. We reach sexual maturity with our first ejaculation or menstruation by age twelve to fourteen and continue to function into our seventies and eighties. Of course sexual activity declines with age, but the degree of satisfaction need not. Most men reach their sexual peak in their teens, nearly ten years before their female counterparts. After that, the penis's angle of erection and degree of hardness steadily declines. The period of time needed to have another erection also grows longer as testosterone levels decrease. After their thirties, most females experience a decrease in vaginal lubrication and orgasms may lessen in intensity, but, like their male partners, they continue to have healthy sex drives. Romance and fantasy still serve as aphrodisiacs, and as partners grow older, experience, patience and the necessity of prolonged foreplay are key in developing intensely intimate sexual relationships. As a result, many couples find greater sexual satisfaction later in life, even if the equipment isn't what it used to be. If we can enjoy fifty or sixty years of good sex, who can complain?

How Do We Have Sex?

Well, if you can imagine it, chances are it has been done. We have sex with our husbands, wives, boyfriends, girlfriends, bosses, employees, strangers, animals, toys and ourselves. People are sexually stimulated by touching, rubbing, kissing, caressing, smelling, sucking, tasting, hearing, hurting, pretending and watching. Methods of intercourse include vaginal, oral, anal and coital positions numbering in the thousands. Granted, some of the above activities are considered deviant, but even so, you must admit that the variety is impressive.

Finally, how long? For the resounding majority of us, sex lasts between fifteen minutes and an hour. So, if you are typical, you may spend about three and a half hours each month having sex. That's forty-two hours a year – less than two days! For a subject that dominates our news, entertainment, conversation, literature and advertising twenty-four hours a day, 365 days a year, you'd think we would devote more time to practising.

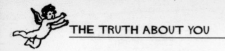

A Brief History of Sex Testing: How We Got Here

The tests chosen for this book originated from needs in society. For example, we saw how intelligence testing became popular in the United States when the army needed to assess the IQs of soldiers, and how creativity testing grew when businesses needed to find creative individuals. In many ways, the study of sexual attitudes is no different. Although psychology has been trying to analyse human sexuality for a century, the complexities of sexual behaviour and our unending interest in the topic means we still have plenty to learn. Early testing on sex focused on the how, the when and the where. More recently, psychology has moved on to the why. The attitudes that steer our behaviour are now under close scrutiny. In 1987, the husband-and-wife psychology team of Clyde and Susan Hendrick saw a need for a comprehensive sex attitudes test that would measure our beliefs. Furthermore, they wanted an easy-to-take test that is applicable to everyone, regardless of sexual orientation or level of experience. It took them several years to get there, but they developed it. Not only will you enjoy taking this next test, but I guarantee you will learn something about yourself.

TAKING THE TEST

This test is easy to take. However, there are forty-three questions and you must give each one some thought. There is no time limit and there are no right or wrong answers. Take this test when you have some quiet time. Use it as an opportunity to learn about yourself. It is also great fun to ask your lover and friends to take this test so you can compare yourself to those closest to you.

TEST YOURSELF

INSTRUCTIONS

This test focuses on your attitudes towards key aspects of sexuality. Take this test at a time when you are comfortable and not distracted. It takes about twenty minutes to complete the questions, but there is no time limit. When you are ready, turn the page and begin. Mark your answers on the page by circling the number that best represents your opinion.

Do not rush through this test. Take your time. Be honest with yourself and have fun!

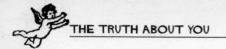

WHAT ARE YOUR SEXUAL OPINIONS?

Indicate below the extent to which you agree or disagree with the following:

1. I do not need to be committed to a person to have sex with him or her.

Strongly Disagree	Disagree	Neutral	Agree	Strongly Agree
1	2	3	4	5

2. Casual sex is acceptable.

1	2	3	4	5

3. I would like to have sex with many partners.

1	2	3	4	5

4. One-night stands are sometimes very enjoyable.

1	2	3	4	5

5. It is okay to have ongoing sexual relationships with more than one person at a time.

1	2	3	4	5

6. It is okay to manipulate someone into having sex as long as no future promises are made.

1	2	3	4	5

7. Sex as a simple exchange of favours is okay if both people agree.

Strongly Disagree	Disagree	Neutral	Agree	Strongly Agree
1	2	3	4	5

8. The best sex is with no strings attached.

1	2	3	4	5

9. Life would have fewer problems if people could have sex more freely.

1	2	3	4	5

10. It is possible to enjoy sex with a person and not like that person very much.

1	2	3	4	5

11. Sex is more fun with someone you don't love.

1	2	3	4	5

12. It is all right to pressure someone into having sex.

1	2	3	4	5

13. Extensive premarital sexual experience is fine.

1	2	3	4	5

14. Extramarital affairs are all right as long as one's partner doesn't know about them.

1	2	3	4	5

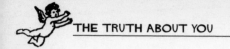

15. Sex for its own sake is perfectly all right.

Strongly Disagree	Disagree	Neutral	Agree	Strongly Agree
1	2	3	4	5

16. I would feel comfortable having intercourse with my partner in the presence of other people.

1	2	3	4	5

17. Prostitution is acceptable.

1	2	3	4	5

18. It is okay for sex to be just good physical release.

1	2	3	4	5

19. Sex without love is meaningless.

5	4	3	2	1

20. People should at least be friends before they have sex together.

5	4	3	2	1

21. In order for sex to be good, it must also be meaningful.

5	4	3	2	1

22. Birth control is part of responsible sexuality.

1	2	3	4	5

23. A woman should share responsibility for birth control.

Strongly Disagree	Disagree	Neutral	Agree	Strongly Agree
1	2	3	4	5

24. A man should share responsibility for birth control.

1	2	3	4	5

25. Sex education is important to young people.

1	2	3	4	5

26. Using 'sex toys' during lovemaking is acceptable.

1	2	3	4	5

27. Masturbation is all right.

1	2	3	4	5

28. Masturbating one's partner during intercourse can increase the pleasure of sex.

1	2	3	4	5

29. Sex gets better as a relationship progresses.

1	2	3	4	5

30. Sex is the closest form of communication between two people.

1	2	3	4	5

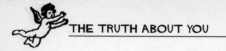
31. A sexual encounter between two people deeply in love is the ultimate human interaction.

Strongly Disagree	Disagree	Neutral	Agree	Strongly Agree
1	2	3	4	5

32. Orgasm is the greatest experience in the world.

1	2	3	4	5

33. At best, sex seems to be the merging of two souls.

1	2	3	4	5

34. Sex is a very important part of my life.

1	2	3	4	5

35. Sex is usually an intensive, almost overwhelming experience.

1	2	3	4	5

36. During sexual intercourse, intense awareness of the partner is the best frame of mind.

1	2	3	4	5

37. Sex is fundamentally good.

1	2	3	4	5

38. Sex is best when you let yourself go and focus on your own pleasure.

Strongly Disagree	Disagree	Neutral	Agree	Strongly Agree
1	2	3	4	5

39. Sex is primarily the taking of pleasure from another person.

1	2	3	4	5

40. The main purpose of sex is to enjoy oneself.

1	2	3	4	5

41. Sex is primarily physical.

1	2	3	4	5

42. Sex is primarily a bodily function, like eating.

1	2	3	4	5

43. Sex is mostly a game between males and females.

1	2	3	4	5

END OF TEST

Susan Hendrick and Clyde Hendrick. 'Multidimensionality of Sexual Attitudes',

Journal of Sex Research, 1987, 23, 502–526. Used by permission.

SCORING YOUR TEST

This is one of those delightfully sneaky tests that tells you a little more about yourself than you really wanted to know. There are four components to your sexual attitude, and each has its own score. To work out your scores, add the following:

PERMISSIVE

This scale measures how sexually liberal you are. The higher your score, the more permissive you are about sex. Calculate your answers to questions 1 to 21 (note the answer categories for items 19, 20 and 21 are deliberately reversed).

Your Permissiveness Score: _____

RESPONSIBLE

This scale measures your tolerance of and responsibility for sexual behaviour. For example, stating that using birth control is part of being sexual shows responsibility. The higher you score, the more sexually responsible you are. Calculate your answers to items 22 to 28 here.

Your Responsibility Score: _____

EMOTIONAL

Many people obtain pleasure from the spiritual aspects of lovemaking. This scale measures the ethereal, emotional aspects where love and sex combine. If you feel that making love is like merging two souls, then you are an emotional lover. Calculate your responses to items 29 to 37.

Your Emotional Score: _____

SELFISH

This aspect of sex measures how sexually selfish you are. Do you have sex solely to satisfy your bodily needs? If so, you probably scored high on this scale. The higher your score, the more of a player you are. Calculate your responses to items 38 to 43.

Your Selfishness Score: _____

UNDERSTANDING YOUR SCORE

Because sex means different things to men and women, we get two scoring charts. For each of your scores, circle the number in the table below closest to your score to see how you compare to others. Keep in mind that the figures presented here were obtained from university students, who may be more liberal in their sexual attitudes than older generations.

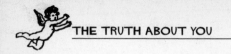

WOMEN'S SCORES

CONSERVATIVE	IRRESPONSIBLE	COLD	GIVING	
–	18	26	–	
20	20	28	6	Low
25	22	30	8	
30	24	32	10	
35	26	34	12	
40	28	36	14	Average
45	30	38	16	
50	32	40	18	
55	34	42	20	
60	36	44	22	High
65	38	46	24	
PERMISSIVE	RESPONSIBLE	EMOTIONAL	SELFISH	

MEN'S SCORES

CONSERVATIVE	IRRESPONSIBLE	COLD	GIVING	
35	18	26	6	
40	20	28	8	Low
45	22	30	10	
50	24	32	12	
55	26	34	14	
60	28	36	16	Average
65	30	38	18	
70	32	40	20	
75	34	42	22	
80	36	44	24	High
85	38	46	26	
PERMISSIVE	RESPONSIBLE	EMOTIONAL	SELFISH	

Now that you have your scores, let's see how your sexual needs and opinions compare to others. To start, check out the numbers you circled above. How far are they from the middle? The middle line indicates the average opinions of hundreds of people who have taken this test. If your attitudes are more unusual, you will have circled numbers nearer the top or bottom of each column. If any of your scores is at the very top or bottom of the table, you are a zealot. Top and bottom scores are only reported by about one in ten people.

As we further delve into your sexual attitudes, we will deal with each aspect of your sexual life one at a time. While the descriptions below focus on your results, it is also extremely interesting to compare your score to your partner's. Generally, similar scores indicate compatibility. This is a key element in a sexual relationship. If you and your partner have scores on any subscales that are widely different, talk about the topics described below. They are likely to be causing some sexual dissatisfaction in your relationship.

PERMISSIVENESS

Sexual permissiveness refers to permitting behaviour that others forbid. There is a range of beliefs over what is permissible and what is illicit. Some people believe that human sexuality is a divine gift and sex is only to be practised within the holy estate of marriage. Others believe that sex is a natural, pleasurable human activity and

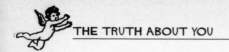

what two consenting adults do is really nobody's business but their own. People who score high on the permissive scale tend to believe that casual sex is acceptable, one-night stands can be great and sex is best when it is approached as a form of physical relief. Low scores shun multiple partners and premarital sex, and feel that for sex to be good it must have meaning.

LOW SCORERS

Straightlaced! You are pretty darn conventional in the bedroom. You are likely to prefer to be in a long-term, monogamous relationship or married before you enjoy sex. You believe that sex without love is not meaningful. When you enter a relationship you quickly look for commitment, but be aware this can be off-putting to potential mates. You also may be slow to warm up to people. You tend to have conservative sexual beliefs and worry too much about what people may be thinking about your behaviour.

MEDIUM SCORERS

At ease! You are comfortable with your sexuality. Your beliefs about sexual permissiveness are right about average. You maintain a healthy balance between your sexy needs and society's norms. You have a healthy mix of adventure and caution and you tend to have few problems finding sexually compatible mates. You enjoy the physical aspects of sex and have an equal appreciation of committed relationships.

HIGH SCORERS

Hot stuff! You are uninhibited and you like your pleasure hot and fast. You crave new experiences and excitement, but tend to become bored quickly. You know what you want and you are tolerant of the desires of others. You probably have had more sexual partners than average. You believe that life would be much simpler if people would have sex more liberally. You are not constrained by societal norms or peer pressure. However, you may have a problem developing meaningful relationships. To form long-lasting bonds, you should devote more time to learning about and developing a history with your partner.

SEXUAL RESPONSIBILITY

There are certain responsibilities that come with sexual activity, including discussing birth control, understanding sexual function and learning ways to please your lover. You can have sex after discussing these topics with your partner or you can blow them off. This is what the sexual responsibility scale measures: how seriously you take being a sexual being.

LOW SCORERS

Hold the phone! You may be an out-of-control lover. You do most of your thinking with the hips. You are more interested in gratification

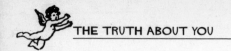

than procreation. Put the sex toys down for a moment. It's time for some learning. Help yourself and spend a little time studying the emotions (and plumbing) of the opposite sex. To be a good lover you must be responsible, careful and caring. It is likely that you are set in your selfish ways, and if so, you'll need some sex education and a patient lover who is willing to teach.

MEDIUM SCORERS

Doing it well. You are on the ball when it comes to being a responsible lover. You are familiar with the physical and emotional aspects of making love and grasp your partner's sexual needs, but there is room for growth. You may benefit from an open and frank dialogue with a lover who practises more responsible lovemaking. If your partner wants you to be more open-minded and take more responsibility for your sexual needs, listen to him/her. You enjoy sexual experimentation and new experiences, but sometimes your inhibitions get in the way.

HIGH SCORERS

Conscientious lover. For you, sex is most satisfying when you are in control. You know your birds and bees. You are tolerant of new experiences and the desires of your partner. Conceivably you most enjoy a varied sex life, you like to try a variety of positions and your partner should be grateful to have you. You know your contraception and you're an informed lover.

EMOTION

There is a calm, unearthly zone where sex and love meet, where one kiss can equal an hour of foreplay and where a silent gaze into your lover's eyes speaks volumes. This is the realm of communion.

LOW SCORERS

You're an animal! Your sexual being is grounded with firm roots in the process of intercourse rather than the spiritual aspects of making love. You have sex, but you don't make love. You (or your partner) may be interested in developing a more sensitive, emotional approach to lovemaking. If your partner wants a little more romance and a little less sweat, please oblige.

MEDIUM SCORERS

You're well rounded. It is said that for men, a happy sex life leads to a happy marriage and that for women, a happy marriage leads to a happy sex life. You agree with this statement and have a balanced attitude towards sex. Sometimes you desire an emotional, spiritual bond with your partner and other times you just want to do the deed. This variability is good. Keep an open dialogue with your partner so he/she knows your mood. Be on the lookout for ways to add romance to the bedroom.

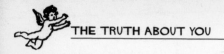

HIGH SCORERS

You're romantic! You are probably deeply in love right now. You view sex as a spiritual combining of two souls. However, you have an emotional, almost fragile, perspective on what sex is about. You are not as interested in the biological basis of sex, as in how it can strengthen your relationship. You are idealistic in this sense. You believe that the more pleasure you can give your partner, the more pleasure you will receive. You are probably very good in bed.

SELFISHNESS

When it comes to sex, you can be a giver or a taker. Do you make love to please your partner or bone like a bad dog to satisfy yourself? Let us see . . .

LOW SCORERS

Giver. You are one of those warm, kind, down-to-earth lovers who values your partner's needs and opinions. To you, sex is not a game but a shared dance of love. You are a sexual 'supplier' who grants pleasure and asks little in return.

MEDIUM SCORERS

Sensibly sensitive. Your sexual desires vary from warm and giving to self-centred and greedy. While sometimes you are excessively concerned with your own satisfaction, you also want your partner to be happy. Strive to be more giving and focus on your partner's pleasure. Overall, you are a pretty good lover.

HIGH SCORERS

User. You may trick and deceive your partner into having sex with you. To you, relationships are games to get sex. You probably do not have fulfilling affairs and your cynical approach to sex causes you to become bored in the bedroom. Wise up – sex is more than a bodily function.

TAKING THE TEST

Now that we know more about your sexual beliefs, we have one more quiz to learn how satisfied you are with your sex life. This test was developed in the 1970s just as the explosion in sex studies began. The author of this one, Joseph LoPiccolo, is a bigwig in sex psychology. He was the president of the Society for the Scientific Study of Sexuality, or SSSS for short. Dr LoPiccolo noticed that there was no good simple assessment device for measuring sexual desires, so he wrote one. This test is a wonderful tool to share with your partner. Or, if you do not currently have a partner, use it to explore your desires.

Dr LoPiccolo wrote this test for heterosexual couples; I have updated a few questions for all couples to use.

TEST YOURSELF

INSTRUCTIONS

This test focuses on your sexual history and desires. This test only takes about ten minutes. Take it when you are comfortable and not distracted. There is no time limit. When you are ready, you may begin. For each of the thirteen questions, write the number that best represents your experience and the number that indicates your wishes most closely.

Do not rush. Be honest with yourself and have fun!

WHAT ARE YOUR SEXUAL EXPERIENCES AND DESIRES?

In the first column, enter the number that corresponds with how often each of these experiences happens to you. In the second column, enter the number that means how often you would like it to happen to you. Use the third column to write the difference between how often it happens and how often you would like it to happen.

POSSIBLE ANSWERS					
1	**2**	**3**	**4**	**5**	**6**
Never	Rarely	Occasionally	Fairly Often	Usually	Always

SEXUAL ACTIVITY	How Often Does This Happen?	How Often Would You Like It to Happen?	Difference
1. Seeing your partner nude.			
2. Your partner seeing you nude.			
3. Kissing for one minute continuously.			
4. Giving your partner a body massage without touching sexual parts.			
5. Your partner giving you a body massage without touching sexual parts.			
6. Caressing your partner's private parts with your hands.			
7. Your partner caressing your private parts with their hands.			
8. Caressing your partner's private parts with your lips or mouth.			

	How Often Does This Happen?	How Often Would You Like It to Happen?	Difference
9. Your partner caressing your private parts with their lips or mouth.			
10. Caressing your partner until he/she reaches orgasm.			
11. Your partner caressing you until you reach orgasm.			
12. Having sexual intercourse.			
13. Having sexual intercourse until you both have an orgasm.			

Totals _____ _____ _____

END OF TEST

J. LoPiccolo and J. Steger, 'The Sexual Interaction Inventory: A New Instrument for Assessment of Sexual Dysfunction'. *Archives of Sexual Behavior,* 1974, 3, 585–595. Reprinted by permission.

Scoring Your Test

It can be difficult to take something warm and loving like your sex life and dissect it into thirteen cold, clinical sections. Then, to top it off, you are asked to put numbers to sex acts! This definitely is not romance, but it is a good objective study of sex. In fact, you have just taken an extremely useful, scientific test.

Scoring is simple. For each item, subtract the smaller number from the bigger number and write in the difference in the third column. This way there are no negative numbers. Then just add up the three columns.

Understanding Your Score

The key to this test is your score on the difference column. This is because you may have a high score in column 1, which means these sexual encounters are happening to you often, but perhaps you don't want them as frequently. Or you may have a lower score on the 'How Often' column and that is just the way you like it. The difference column tells you if you are getting what you want. We will focus on that.

The lower your score, the more satisfied you are with your sexual experiences.

Difference Scores of 0–7. Nirvana, here we come!

You are extremely satisfied with your sex life. You and your lover probably have excellent communication skills, you let each other know what you like and dislike – and how often you like it. Be sure to test your partner too. If your partner also scored between zero and seven you are a wonderful lover. Keep up the communication and you will enjoy many happy years of great sex.

Difference Scores of 8–13. Oooh la la!

You have a fulfilled sex life. You and your partner probably have wonderful communication skills, you let each other know what you like and dislike – and generally how often you like them. You may differ on a couple of activities, but make sure your partner takes this test and discuss your results together. Continue to communicate and you'll enjoy many happy years of good sex.

Difference Scores of 14–39. Close, but no cigar!

You are close to sexual bliss, but you and your partner have some work to do. You are either not letting your partner clearly know your needs or your partner is not doing his/her job to fulfil those needs. Talk about this test with your lover. Read through your partner's answers. If your mate's score is similar to yours, you both have homework. Schedule some romantic time together and talk about your needs and wishes. Be flexible and help your partner get a lower score too. Both of you should focus on improving your communication and retake this test in a month. Chart your progress.

Difference Scores Above 40. Warning.

Your lover is not meeting your needs. You are sexually unfulfilled. You are not enjoying what you want most of the time. There may be problems in your relationship other than lack of sexual satisfaction. Talk about this test with your partner. Read through your lover's answers. Study the ideas at the end of this chapter. Take some tips from the relationship chapter too.

How Do You Compare?

Now that we have thoroughly measured your sexual attitudes and satisfaction, let's see how you compare to other people. These comparisons are organised by the various stages of our sexual lives.

ARE YOU A VIRGIN?

If so, you are considered to be quite a sexual catch – regardless of your gender. Contrary to popular belief, both men and women find that little or no sexual experience is an appealing attribute in a potential mate. Also, if you have some sexual experience as a part of a committed, loving relationship, give yourself a gold star. Men and women who have sexual relations in a close partnership are seen as preferred dates, more desirable potential spouses and less aggressive than those with a bedpost scarred with notches. People perceived as having many sexual partners or having sex in noncommited

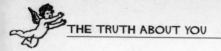

relationships are viewed as less moral, less likeable, and generally less well adjusted.

WHEN DID YOU START HAVING SEX?

Most of us lose our virginity between the ages of fifteen and twenty-two. By age fifteen, about 15 per cent of us have had our first sexual experience. By seventeen over half are no longer virgins, and by the time we are twenty-two years old, 90 per cent of us have become sexually experienced. However, there is some cultural variation in the average age of first intercourse. Black men report being the youngest, with about half being sexually experienced by age fifteen. Conversely, Hispanic women claim losing their virginity the latest. About half of all Hispanic women report their first sexual experience at 18 years. The table below provides a breakdown of intercourse experience by race and ethnicity for Americans:

AGE BY WHICH 50 PER CENT OF POPULATION

HAVE HAD FIRST INTERCOURSE

Black Men	15 years
Black Women	16½ years
Hispanic Men	16½ years
White Men	17 years
White Women	17½ years
Hispanic Women	18 years

Here is another little titbit. The decision of how soon couples have sex after starting their relationship is made almost solely by the woman. Women tend to consider their religious beliefs, sexual history and hopes for the relationship before committing to sex. Although most men apply pressure to begin having sex, they have almost no say in when the relationship turns sexual. The women wear the pants on this one.

WHY DID YOU START HAVING SEX?
When couples decide to have intercourse for the first time, the reasons they do it are as old as gender differences themselves.

WHY DID YOU DECIDE TO FIRST HAVE SEX?

	MEN	WOMEN
Curiosity	51%	24%
Affection for Partner	25	48
Physical Pleasure	12	3
Wedding Night	7	21
Peer Pressure	4	3

HOW MANY SEX PARTNERS HAVE YOU HAD?
First, let's address some myths. Americans are not sex-craving lunatics hopping into bed with strangers, poor people are no more permissive than the wealthy and race is not a significant factor in the number of sexual partners one has. In fact, the vast majority of

us, regardless of race, religion and education, are monogamous. Over 80 per cent of us have had one or zero partners in the past year. But as the old adage goes, *sex sells*. Our boring sex lives don't make for good commercials, and people are often distressed about how little sex they have.

If we look at the number of sex partners we have over our entire life, the picture is tame. Almost 30 per cent of American adults have had one or zero sexual partners. Another 30 per cent have had between two and four. About a quarter have had five to ten partners and one in five report having over ten partners.

HOW DOES YOUR MATE MEASURE UP?

We saw on page 3 that early scientists measured the toes of prostitutes in the name of science. Now over one hundred years later, you can see how science has progressed.

Biologist John Manning from the University of Liverpool measured the *fingers* of men and women to determine whether relative finger length points to fertility. He found that men tend to have higher levels of testosterone in their blood if their ring finger is longer than their index finger. Women, however, are different. They have higher levels of oestrogen if their index finger is longer than their ring finger.

Manning also suggests that this is why women go gaga over musicians. He measured the hands of seventy symphony musicians and found that these guys tend to have longer ring fingers too. So, ladies, look at your man's hands and see if there is a ring of truth to these studies.

ARE YOU SEXUALLY PERMISSIVE?

If you scored high on the permissive scale, chances are you fall into several of these categories:

Sexually Permissive People Also Tend to Be:

Younger. Each generation tends to be a little more permissive than its predecessor and, as we age, we tend to become more sexually conservative.

Educated. The longer you have been in school, the more permissive you tend to be.

Happy. People who describe themselves as generally 'pretty happy' tend to be more sexually tolerant. Interestingly, those who identify themselves as 'very happy' tend to be less permissive.

Less Religious. Those with no religious affiliation and poor church attendance are significantly more lenient in the bedroom.

City Slickers. Rural and small town dwellers tend to be traditional compared to city slickers.

Worldly. People who tend to have a world view, as opposed to a more parochial perspective, tend to be less puritanical.

ARE YOU A PRUDE?

Even in the twenty-first century, there are many social mores that

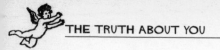

penalise women for being sexually assertive. Those who initiate conversations with men and invite them out to dinner are perceived as acting in a less socially acceptable manner. Psychologists Elizabeth Allgeier and Alan Fogel took this idea down the path of sexuality. They showed volunteers a slide show of women engaged in 'traditional' (missionary) and 'nontraditional' (women on top) coital positions. What did people say about the slide show? Females were particularly critical of the women photographed. They rated the participants in the nontraditional shots as dirty, less respectable, less moral, not good and less desirable as wives and mothers compared to the women enjoying traditional missionary positions. There you have it: in American society, women can be their own worst enemies.

IS YOUR MATE THE PERFECT FATHER?

Let's face it, the purpose of sex is to have children, but what if you could pick the perfect father of your child? Would you pick someone different from your mate? Turns out, for many women the answer is yes. Joanna Scheib and her colleagues had a clever idea: they asked young women to pretend they were selecting a sperm donor. Scheib asked women in Canada and Norway what they looked for in their hypothetical donor compared to what they looked for in a long-term mate. When choosing a sperm donor, women carefully considered characteristics such as health, intelligence, creativity, musical ability and attractiveness. When choosing a mate, character traits such as kindness, understanding, dependability, consideration, affection, honesty and self-confidence were seen as more important, along with the ability to earn income.

It makes sense. If you are going to spend the rest of your life with someone, you want character traits you can live with. But in your children, good health, intelligence and talent are more desirable. So, fellas, look at it this way, if you fail the character tests in this book, don't fret – you can still be a sperm donor.

HOW DOES HE COMPARE?

- The average adult penis is three to four inches long when flaccid.

- While penises range in size from one to ten inches long when erect, most are between five and seven inches long. The average is about six inches – that is about as long as a ballpoint pen.

- The maximum diameter of the average penis grows about a quarter of an inch to one and one-half inches. That is about the width of a tube of toothpaste.

- A man's build or race is not related to the size and shape of his penis.

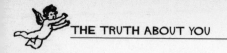

ARE YOU WELL EDUCATED?

Considering going to university? You may want to rethink that decision. According to the National Center for Health Statistics, the more education you have, the less intercourse you have. The question of *why* this is the case is not known. There are three possibilities being debated:

1. Educated people take fewer chances and are less sexually adventurous.
2. It takes time to be educated, so degreed people tend to be older and less sexually active.
3. People with advance degrees have more headaches (according to the American Medical Association).

DO YOU POSTPONE SEX BECAUSE OF HEADACHES?

If you put off sex because you have a headache, you should think again. According to the London School of Hygiene and Tropical Medicine, the endorphins your body produces during sex are just as powerful as aspirin.

DO YOU KNOW YOUR SEXUAL CHEMISTRY?

There is a wonderful little hormone that drives us wild with desire. It is oxytocin. Oxytocin is the drug that promotes contractions during childbirth, makes new mothers secrete milk and makes mothers want to hug their children. It has been called the 'cuddle chemical'. The good news is that oxytocin is not just for mothers and children; it is also for husbands and wives. During lovemaking our brains secrete this lushly pleasurable substance, which in turn excites the nerve endings in our genitals and causes them to fire at will. These sensations cause us to have orgasms. Also, one of the other great actions of oxytocin is that your body will pump it out in response to either physical or emotional cues. Like Pavlov and his dogs, a certain gaze from your partner or the sound of your lover's voice can start the tide of this love drug flowing.

Because women are more susceptible to the seduction of oxytocin, they prefer to cuddle after orgasm. Furthermore, while men produce five times their normal levels of oxytocin during sex, women produce even more. This mother's little helper helps women achieve multiple orgasms.

How Does She Compare?

- Breast size has no effect on milk production. Breast size is primarily determined by the amount of fat surrounding the milk glands.

- A woman who nurses a child for six months can produce over forty gallons of milk.

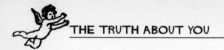

- Shortly before orgasm, 75 per cent of women experience a sex flush during which a quick rash appears on their breasts, chest, neck and head.

HOW OFTEN DO YOU MAKE LOVE?

We are seemingly obsessed with sex. We are surrounded by constant reminders of the sexual good life. Advertising is replete with subtle sexual messages, double entendres are the staple for many conversations and sex has been the major theme in popular music for the last forty years. But you may be surprised to learn that we read and think about it much more than we do it. Overall, the average American has sex once a week. But no one is average. Sex is like wealth – it is not distributed evenly. The sexiest 15 per cent of the nation gets half the intercourse. Twenty per cent of us got no sex in the past year. Only 5 per cent are doing it three times a week or more. No wonder we want to read about it and see it on television: for most of us, sex is a novelty.

WHO HAS THE MOST SEX?

You have heard of the expression 'money can't buy happiness'. Now I'm here to tell you that money will not lead to more sex, either. In fact, men earning more than £40,000 have about 20 per cent *less* sex than those earning about £16,000. What other characteristics do the most sexually active share? According to a national survey of ten thousand Americans, those who have the most sex:

- have some college education, but no degree
- do not attend religious services
- have two or more children
- are in their early twenties
- approve of pornography
- watch public television
- are politically liberal
- work long hours

Sound like anybody you know?

DO YOU HAVE A SEXUALLY ACTIVE PERSONALITY?
Your personality may also provide clues to how often you have sex. The following traits are associated with whether you have sex early and often:

Tends to Be Sexually Active	Tends to Be Sexually Inert
Dominant	Deferential
Persuasive	Disheartened
Gregarious	Levelheaded
Affectionate	Aloof
Cheery	Gloomy
Adventurous	Apprehensive
Optimistic	Pessimistic
Extroverted	Introverted

DO YOU LIKE JAZZ?

If you are a jazz fan, chances are you are having 30 per cent more sex than everyone else. That's right, jazz is the music of love. Fondness for other types of music, including rock and rap, has no bearing on the frequency of sex.

DO YOU SPEAK THE LANGUAGE OF LOVE?

Now, you don't need me to tell you that men and women are different, but I do have to tell you about this quickie experiment. Pretend you are walking across your average university campus and an attractive stranger of the opposite sex comes up to you and says: 'I have been noticing you around campus and I find you very attractive.' Then the stranger asks one of three questions: 'Would you go out with me tonight?' 'Would you come over to my flat tonight?' or 'Would you go to bed with me tonight?' What would you say?

The first thing you may ask is, 'Is this one of those weird psychology experiments I have been reading about?' However, the fact is that your gender greatly influences your reply. See how your answers compared to kids on campus:

	PER CENT RESPONDING 'YES'	
AN ATTRACTIVE STRANGER ASKS YOU . . .	Men	Women
Would you go out with me tonight?	50%	56%
Would you come over to my flat tonight?	69%	6%
Would you go to bed with me tonight?	75%	0%

DO YOU LIKE GRAHAM CRACKERS?

Many Americans love graham crackers (similar to our digestive biscuits), but relatively few know that in 1829 Dr Sylvester Graham, a minister, invented them to cure masturbation! He believed that certain foods excited the genitalia, and encouraged people to adopt a more bland diet. An ardent vegetarian and leader of the temperance movement, Dr Graham believed the coarsely ground wheat flour would calm the genitals of young people. Incidentally, he also believed that consuming animals led to 'sexual incontinence'.

SEXUAL MYTHS...

So you think you know how this sex thing works? Have a look at what we used to believe . . .

- Babies came from minute particles given off by stars that float down to earth and land in women's wombs.

- Men's testicles contain sperm to make boys on one side and sperm to make girls on the other.

- If a man has a large nose, he has a large penis.

- If a man has large feet, he has a small penis.

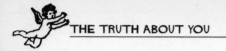

- A woman with a large mouth has a large vagina.

- A woman can make a man fall in love with her by tricking him into drinking some of her menstrual blood.

- Eating horse testicles makes men virile.

- Eating kangaroo testicles makes women aroused.

WANT TO IMPROVE YOUR SEX LIFE?

Many people mistakenly judge the quality of sex by the quantity of their partner's orgasms. What they fail to realise is that the crucial element for a good sex life is communication. You must effectively tell your partner what you want. And you must listen and share your partner's preferences. Couples who share their sexual desires and cooperate in pleasing each other have intercourse more frequently and find sex more satisfying. If you are unsure of how to let your partner know what you want, and need some help communicating your needs, try giving off these sexual signals:

- *Let's try this.* Tell your partner what you like and don't like. To be a good lover you may occasionally do some awkward things to please your partner. This is being giving and loving. But if your partner is trying to please you and they are not quite doing what you like – let them know. A quiet whisper of 'harder', 'softer', 'faster' or 'slower' puts you on the right track for more communication. Alternatively, you don't always need words. Take control and guide your partner's hands, mouth or body to where you want it. Don't just say you don't like that, give your partner an alternative you can both enjoy.

- *I want to have sex!* If you scored higher on the difference column, there may be times when your partner might not know it is show time. You may have to be blunt. Light some candles in the bedroom, turn off the lights and TV, and lead your partner into bed. If your partner is not tuned into your needs, take some initiative. If your partner is not in the mood, do not make a production out of it. Assure them that is fine and let him/her know that you are ready when they are.

- *A whisper away from bed.* Good sexual communication is not limited to the bedroom. Choose an unguarded moment to let your significant other know something special. Perhaps while making dinner you can whisper in your partner's ear: 'I sure do like it when you . . .' Or while your partner is doing a chore like washing the dishes, take control, let them know that you will take care of the dishes tonight because your partner needs to save their energy for later.

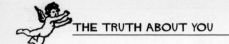

- *Surprise.* Plan a day together with no distractions. Take the phone off the hook and keep the TV off. Do something you both enjoy together. Go for a hike or ride a bike, paint a room or work on a hobby. The great thing about working on a project or hobby together is that women often say they miss conversation with their men and men often report they miss doing things with their lady. With activities like these, he gets the action, she gets a chat and maybe even your home gets spruced up. It can also lead to other . . . more enjoyable . . . activities.

Sometimes even with a wonderful relationship and great communication, sex can become dull or routine. Once you have mastered communication, there are other activities you can do to spice up your sex life. The suggestions below start mild and quickly get zesty:

- *Kiss Your Lover.* It may sound obvious, but you would be surprised at how many couples skip this important step. A peck in the morning and at night is not going to cut it. Give your lover a good long kiss often. Let them know how you feel. Touch your partner. A gentle pat on the bottom or shoulder rub while washing dishes quietly speaks volumes.

- *Schedule Romance.* Don't wait for spontaneity. If you have children or a busy career, you end up waiting a long time. Plan trysts you enjoy.

- *Pay Attention to the Little Things.* Buy her some flowers for no reason. Write him a little note and put it by his toothbrush or in his car. Leave a sexy message on your lover's answering machine. It is the small treats in day-to-day life that inspire romance.

- *Keep Your Bedroom Private.* Do not use it as an office or for family gatherings. Do not bring work, family or daily woes into the bedroom.

- *Make Time.* Call in late for work and start the day cuddling together. Or plan a lunch rendezvous with your lover at home. If you have children, make sure they go to bed early enough so you have some together time. Turn off the TV and look at the stars, have a stroll or take a bath together. Make some time together away from the hassles of work and children.

- *Create a Sexual Wish List.* Both you and your partner each write a list of five different sexual acts you would like to explore. Be honest with each other, form a pact to explore these desires, then read each other's lists. Jot down a sexual fantasy you have always had but have never acted out.

- *Create a Non-sexual Wish List.* Form the same agreement as above and write a list of five non-sexual, romantic desires in which you would like to participate.

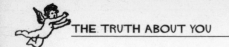

- *Role Play.* You and your partner take ten slips of paper. Write down the names of five women and five men you both know. The names can be mutual friends, celebrities or famous people from history, but no relatives. Or write down the names of different occupations and play doctor and nurse, teacher and principal, or handyman and needy housewife. Place the slips of paper into cups. Light some candles in the bedroom, pull out two names and explore your new partner.

- *Mystery Role Play.* Recreate history with tantalising liaisons such as those that might have taken place between Elvis Presley and Bonnie Parker, Caesar and Amelia Earhart or Henry VIII and Mary Poppins. There are many fun things you can do with this game; for example, don't tell your partner who you are and dress and act the part. Crank up your imagination and let your body go.

- *Have a Silent Night.* Spend a romantic evening together without uttering a word to each other. Use your imagination to make all of your communication non-verbal. For example, use gestures, facial expressions, and move your partner's hands to express your thoughts. No writing notes and definitely no talking (although grunts and groans are permitted).

- *Try New Locations.* You don't need to take a cruise to the Caribbean to enjoy sex in a new spot. Try doing it in a different room or closet, outside, or in the car (even parked in the garage!). Use your imagination and make love on a table, chair or sofa.

5
HAPPINESS

Remember that happiness is a way of travel –
not a destination.

ROY M. GOODMAN, U.S. SENATOR

The study of happiness used to be solely in the domain of poets and philosophers. Now psychologists have joined the fray, dissecting happiness and studying its pieces. How happy are you? What makes you happy? How can you become happier? Happiness, or 'subjective well-being', as psychologists often refer to it, is a tricky concept to quantify. You may have fleeting moments of joy throughout your day, but how do you measure the amount of happiness in your life?

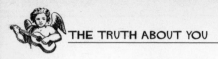

WHAT IS HAPPINESS?

Happiness can be that first taste of ice cream on a hot summer day, or the pleasure felt when you look back over your life and reminisce about the good times. We all experience brief moments of elation. These moments may be just a smile for a few seconds or a momentary laugh. It can be a chuckle brought on by the antics of another or the satisfaction of helping a friend.

Happiness is something we all need, but few of us are content with the amount we have. While we try to make ourselves happy in many ways, its elusive nature often leaves our efforts unfulfilled. At the same time, happiness has an odd habit of sneaking up when you least expect it. Though happiness may be the easiest emotion to feel, looking for happiness is a sure way not to find it. Our happiest moments are often sudden and unexpected. Ogden Nash said it best: 'The most exciting happiness is the happiness generated by forces beyond your control.'

Happiness is an important gauge to let our bodies know that all biological and psychological systems are satisfied. Just like hunger tells us it is time to eat and fear tells us there is something dangerous ahead, happiness is our internal monitor that tells us when everything is rosy. But it is more than an on/off switch. Inside each of us there is a sensitive mechanism that detects *types* of unhappiness. For example, a body realises that it is unhappy because of loneliness rather than envy, or insomnia rather than hunger. This 'happiness

mechanism' must pinpoint the cause of the displeasure so the afflicted individual can address the problem and be happy once again. Of course, the system is not fail-safe. People can misdiagnose their misery or trick their bodies into euphoria by alcohol, narcotics and other antidepressant drugs.

THE BIG PICTURE

Now that we know more about what happiness is, we are going to focus on the most important aspect of it: your subjective well-being, or how happy you are with your entire life. The focus of this chapter is not on the temporary pleasures in life but on the universal sense that you are content. Some people make a mistake here. You probably know someone who is looking for Mr Right or hoping to win the lottery. This person wrongly believes that a major life change is going to come along and save him or her from their misery. Unfortunately, the big event almost never happens. Happiness seldom comes from a big change; it comes from the accumulation of many small joys. These small episodes add up to a much more powerful factor in achieving long-term happiness. So do yourself a favour – take the little joys in life and cherish them, and promptly forget the nuisances.

Take a look at what you need and don't need to be happy:

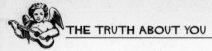

Happiness *Doesn't* Need:

- Beauty

- Status and possessions

- Fame

- Wealth and power

- Special talent

- Intelligence

- Perfectionism

- Conformity

Happiness *Does* Need:

- Self-esteem: happy people like themselves

- Loving relationships and friends

- Optimism: happy people have positive expectations

- Purpose: happy people have goals and believe that their life has a purpose

- A job or activities you enjoy

- Wisdom

- Realism: accepting weaknesses and managing them

- Autonomy: happy people resist social pressure, exert personal control and accept themselves as who they are

Happiness *Doesn't* Need:	Happiness *Does* Need:
▪ Stagnation	▪ Growth: happy people learn about themselves and use that knowledge to realise their potential

We should all breathe a collective sigh of relief after reading these lists. Why? Look at the lists again. The things in life we cannot change have no effect on our happiness, while the traits that help us become happy can all be changed. Our happiness is not dependent on our immutable circumstances; rather, it depends on how we respond to them. Psychologists have discovered that happiness is not a mood or an emotion but a way of living. It is an outlook on life that you can control and manage.

A Brief History of Happiness Testing

While philosophical discussions on happiness probably began with the first language, psychologists did not start to study and measure it until the 1950s. These early studies began with societal comparisons between countries after World War II. But it took another twenty years for this line of research to grow. The 1970s were a time of smiling faces and 'feeling groovy' in North America and Europe. The pursuit of happiness was openly discussed and a few

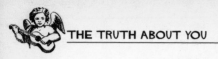

studies were conducted. Happiness research really took off in the late 1980s as a postmaterialistic spirit grew. People grew less satisfied with the things they bought and grew more concerned with living a meaningful life. At the same time, some psychologists grew weary of studying what is wrong with people (like depression, anxiety and stress). They wanted to learn what was right with them – hence the field of subjective well-being.

Taking the Tests

There have been several useful scales developed to measure our subjective well-being. After reviewing them, it became clear that I could provide you with a short story of your own happiness by offering four quizzes. The first is perhaps the easiest to take. It was developed by Dr Ed Diener, a psychologist who is one of the foremost authorities on subjective well-being. The test, called the Satisfaction with Life Scale, only takes a few minutes to complete. However, just because this quiz is quick does not mean it is weak. You will be asked some weighty questions on the following pages and you must evaluate your entire life. This test measures one extremely important thing – how happy you are with your life.

After that we have a real treat: measures of your cheerfulness – one for you *and* one for a friend to complete about you. These tests were devised by Austrian psychologist Willibald Ruch. When it

comes to humour, Willibald wrote the book on it. Seriously! He is coeditor of *Humor Research,* an editor for the *International Journal of Humor Research* and the president of the International Society for Humor Studies.

Finally, we have a test that measures those rare, magical moments of awe-inspiring happiness called 'peak experiences'. The peak experience scale will determine how frequently you experience a sense of oneness with the world. This test was developed by psychologist Dr Eugene Mathes and his colleagues. Dr Mathes has been working in the field of social and personality psychology for over thirty years. We'll cover more of the happiness climax later. Let's start with your satisfaction with life now.

TEST YOURSELF

INSTRUCTIONS

The test you are about to take consists of five questions. It only takes a few minutes to complete, but don't rush. There is no time limit; take as much time as you need. Be open and honest with yourself as you answer each question.

Answer the questions on the test sheet on the next page.

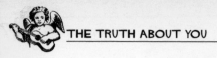

HAPPINESS TEST

For each statement, please use the following seven-point scale where 1 means you strongly disagree with the statement and 7 means you strongly agree with the statement. Indicate your level of agreement with each item by circling the appropriate number.

1. In most ways, my life is close to my ideal.

Strongly Disagree	Disagree	Slightly Disagree	Neutral	Slightly Agree	Agree	Strongly Agree
1	2	3	4	5	6	7

2. The conditions of my life are excellent.

1	2	3	4	5	6	7

3. I am satisfied with my life.

1	2	3	4	5	6	7

4. So far, I have gained the important things I want in life.

1	2	3	4	5	6	7

5. If I could live my life over, I would change almost nothing.

1	2	3	4	5	6	7

END OF TEST

Add the numbers you circled and record your score here _____

William Pavot and Ed Diener, 'Review of the Satisfaction with Life Scale'.
Psychological Assessment, 1993, 5, 2, 164–172. Used by permission.

SCORING YOUR TEST

Scoring this test is simple. Add the five numbers you circled and write your score on the test page.

UNDERSTANDING YOUR SCORE

Before we analyse your happiness score, there are some key concepts to understand. I will be using the terms *pleasant effect, unpleasant effect* and *happiness filter* to help explain how you can increase your happiness. These terms are described as follows:

Pleasant effect means experiencing the emotions that are needed to cause happiness, like affection, pride, gratification and delight. You may increase this effect by changing your outlook on life and taking satisfaction in life's little treats. Enjoy the small things like looking at a piece of artwork, a beautiful sunset or even a favourite old movie.

Unpleasant effect means strong emotions like guilt, melancholy, anger and remorse that deny you the pleasures of life. To reduce unpleasant effects, overlook the negative experiences of the past and live for the moment. If the present has you down, think about a time when you were happier and view life in the long term. Instead of being despondent over what you are missing in life, be grateful for what you have. Try these techniques: be kind to someone who is unkind; don't criticise anyone for twenty-four hours; be more confident.

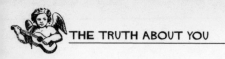

Your brain is constantly making subconscious decisions about whether the experiences in your life are good or bad. Your *happiness filter* is a mechanism that acts like a lens through which you view the world. For our purposes, we will describe three colours: blue, clear and rosy.

For example: You are walking down the street, and a stranger, while leaving a store, drops a carton of milk. The container bursts open, splashing the contents on its owner as well as on your new suede shoes. The stranger apologises.

If your happiness filter is blue, you are mortified by your bad luck. You respond with a stern look and stomp away without saying anything. Throughout the day, you fume about how careless and clumsy the perpetrator was, how you wish you had given the idiot a piece of your mind and how foolish it was to have purchased suede shoes, since they now may be ruined by such a chance encounter. The milk has spoiled your day.

If your filter is clear, you tell the shopper, 'It's all right,' and you look at your shoes and decide to let the milk dry before attempting to clean them. You forget about the incident until that evening when you notice that the white spots have already dried, flaked off and disappeared. This good fortune makes you happy.

If you are the rosy type, you comfort the stranger by laughing and relating how clumsy *you* can be. You help clean up the mess while making casual small talk and enjoying a moment's break from your routine. Later, you tell a friend about the incident and

have another chuckle. The incident remains in your memory as one of those comically awkward encounters that people share.

WHAT DOES YOUR SCORE MEAN?

Score of 5 to 14.
You are dissatisfied with how you are living your life. You are unhappy because you are not getting what you want, perhaps due to a lack of love, friendship, or an inability to take pleasure in entertaining or amusing activities. You are not getting enough *pleasant effect* and are probably experiencing too much *unpleasant effect*.

Your *happiness filter* is probably tinted blue. You may be viewing events in your life more negatively than you should. Try to look at the lighter side of reality rather than crying over spilled milk.

Extra Low Scorers: If you scored between 5 and 9, you are extremely dissatisfied with your life. Seriously focus on improving your happiness by speaking to others. Decide what makes you happy and then explore it. Realise that your behaviour has meaning. If you want happiness, you are going to have to work for it. You must discover the root of your unhappiness and work toward finding a resolution. I lost my wonderful wife of twenty years due to depression; trust me, if you have a low score, tell your loved ones and get professional help.

Review your answers on the test and contemplate what you can do to improve each score. If, for example, you have not attained the important things you want in life (question 4), write down what those things are and work out a strategy to get them. However, be realistic about your goals. Even the happiest people do not have everything they want.

Score of 15 to 25.

You are mildly happy with your life. Work at increasing the amount of pleasure you get from others: listen more, talk less, do good deeds, take long walks, be kind to strangers. Make yourself smile whether you feel like it or not.

In order to become happier, you must take charge: reduce *unpleasant effects,* increase *pleasant effects* and improve those areas that give you satisfaction. Be conscious of your *happiness filter* and go out of your way to be more rosy. See The Path to Greater Happiness at the end of this chapter.

Score of 26 to 31.

You are a happy person. You have a sense of humour, and you like to laugh. You tend to have a clear to rosy outlook and see the positive side of things. Don't stop here – increase your happiness by taking charge of the aspects of your life that cause unhappiness. Chapter 6 also has insights that will help you.

Score of 31 to 35.

Congratulations! You are extremely happy. You see obstacles as challenges and enjoy tackling problems as much as any new experience; you take bad situations and make them good. Your rosy attitude makes you great fun at parties and even more valued in difficult circumstances. Co-workers respect you and enjoy your company.

Now that we have a general sense of how satisfied you are with life, let's delve a little deeper and measure your temperament. Are you good-humoured or ill-humoured? Are you the cheerful type? The next few minutes will tell all.

TEST YOURSELF

INSTRUCTIONS

The test you are about to take consists of thirty questions. It only takes a few minutes to complete, but don't rush. There is no time limit. The statements provided refer to your moods and temperament in general. Refer to your typical behaviour and circle the number that best represents your opinions.

Answer every question on the next five pages.

CHEERFULNESS TEST

For each statement, please use the following four-point scale where 1 means you strongly disagree with the statement and 4 means you strongly agree with the statement. Indicate your level of agreement with each item by circling the appropriate number. Answer every question.

1. Everyday life often gives me the occasion to laugh.

Strongly Disagree   Strongly Agree
    1   2   3   4

2. I prefer people who communicate with deliberation and objectivity.

            1   2   3   4

3. I am a rather sad person.

            1   2   3   4

4. I can easily unwind and enjoy the moment.

            1   2   3   4

5. One of my principles is 'first work, then play'.

            1   2   3   4

6. I am often sullen.

            1   2   3   4

7. Many adversities of everyday life actually do have a positive side.

Strongly Disagree			Strongly Agree
1	2	3	4

8. I am a serious person.

1	2	3	4

9. When friends try to cheer me up by joking or fooling around, I sometimes become more morose and grumpy.

1	2	3	4

10. I often smile.

1	2	3	4

11. In everything I do, I always consider every possible effect and compare all pros and cons carefully.

1	2	3	4

12. There are many days on which I think, 'I got up on the wrong side of the bed.'

1	2	3	4

13. I am often in a joyous mood.

1	2	3	4

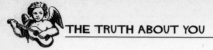

14. In most situations, I initially see the serious aspect.

Strongly Disagree			Strongly Agree
1	2	3	4

15. Even if there is no reason, I often feel ill-humoured.

1	2	3	4

16. I like to laugh and do it often.

1	2	3	4

17. When I communicate with other people, I always try to have an objective and sober exchange of ideas.

1	2	3	4

18. I am often in a bad mood.

1	2	3	4

19. I feel completely contented being with cheerful people.

1	2	3	4

20. When I watch TV, I prefer informative to 'shallow' programmes.

1	2	3	4

21. I often feel despondent.

1	2	3	4

22. Laughing has a contagious effect on me.

Strongly Disagree			Strongly Agree
1	2	3	4

23. I try to spend my free time doing things as useful as possible.

       1   2   3   4

24. I often feel so gloomy that nothing can make me laugh.

       1   2   3   4

25. I am a cheerful person.

       1   2   3   4

26. My everyday life is filled mainly with important things and matters.

       1   2   3   4

27. Some annoying circumstances are capable of spoiling my mood for quite a while.

       1   2   3   4

28. It is easy for me to spread good cheer.

       1   2   3   4

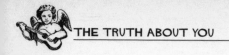

29. When I am in contact with others, I often find that I have thought many things through more thoroughly than they.

Strongly Disagree			Strongly Agree
1	2	3	4

30. Sometimes I am distressed for a very long time.

1	2	3	4

END OF TEST

Willibald Ruch, Gabriele Kohler and Christoph van Thriel, 'Assessing the "Humorous Temperament": Construction of the Facet and Standard Trait Forms of the State-Trait-Cheerfulness-Inventory – STCI'. *Humor: International Journal of Humor Research,* 1996, 9, 303–339. Used by permission.

CHEERFULNESS TEST FOR A FRIEND TO COMPLETE ABOUT YOU

INSTRUCTIONS

A friend has asked you to complete this thirty-question quiz about him/her. The test only takes a few minutes, but don't rush. There is no time limit. The statements provided refer to your friend's moods and temperament in general. Because we cannot always know the thoughts and feelings of others, some questions refer to your *impressions* of your friend.

Don't think too long on these questions – it is best to give your immediate impression. Answer every question and have fun thinking about someone special.

CHEERFULNESS TEST FOR YOUR FRIEND

As you think about each statement, mentally insert your friend's first name in the blank line (_____). Answer each one using the following four-point scale where 1 means you strongly disagree with the statement and 4 means you strongly agree with the statement. Indicate your level of agreement with each item by circling the appropriate number. Answer every question.

1. Everyday life often gives _____ the occasion to laugh.

Strongly Disagree			Strongly Agree
1	2	3	4

---

2. _____ prefers people who communicate with deliberation and objectivity.

1	2	3	4

---

3. _____ is a rather sad person.

1	2	3	4

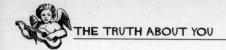
4. _____ can easily unwind and enjoy the moment.

Strongly Disagree   **Strongly Agree**

     1   2   3   4

5. One of _____ 's principles is: 'First work, then play.'

     1   2   3   4

6. _____ is often sullen.

     1   2   3   4

7. _____ seems to think: 'Many adversities of everyday life actually do have a positive side.'

     1   2   3   4

8. _____ is a serious person.

     1   2   3   4

9. When friends try to cheer _____ up by joking or fooling around, he/she sometimes becomes more morose and grumpy.

     1   2   3   4

10. _____ often smiles.

     1   2   3   4

11. In everything _____ does, he/she always considers every possible effect and compares all pros and cons carefully.

Strongly Disagree			**Strongly Agree**
1	2	3	4

12. There are many days on which _____ seems to think. 'I got up on the wrong side of the bed.'

1	2	3	4

13. _____ is often in a joyous mood.

1	2	3	4

14. In most situations, _____ initially sees the serious aspect.

1	2	3	4

15. Even if there is no reason, _____ often feels ill-humoured.

1	2	3	4

16. _____ likes to laugh and does it often.

1	2	3	4

17. When _____ communicates with other people, he/she always tries to have an objective and sober exchange of ideas.

1	2	3	4

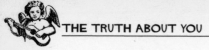

18. _____ is often in a bad mood.

	Strongly Disagree			Strongly Agree
	1	**2**	**3**	**4**

19. _____ seems to be completely contented being with cheerful people.

1	**2**	**3**	**4**

20. When _____ watches TV, he/she prefers informative reports to 'shallow' programmes.

1	**2**	**3**	**4**

21. _____ often feels despondent.

1	**2**	**3**	**4**

22. Laughing has a contagious effect on _____.

1	**2**	**3**	**4**

23. _____ tries to spend his/her free time doing things as useful as possible.

1	**2**	**3**	**4**

24. _____ often seems to feel so gloomy that nothing can make him/her laugh.

1	**2**	**3**	**4**

25. _____ is a cheerful person.

Strongly Disagree			Strongly Agree
1	2	3	4

26. _____'s everyday life is filled mainly with important things and matters.

1	2	3	4

27. Some annoying circumstances are capable of spoiling _____'s mood for quite a while.

1	2	3	4

28. It is easy for _____ to spread good cheer.

1	2	3	4

29. When _____ is in contact with others, he/she often seems to find that he/she thought many things through more thoroughly than they.

1	2	3	4

30. Sometimes _____ is distressed for a very long time.

1	2	3	4

END OF TEST

Willibald Ruch, Gabriele Kohler and Christoph van Thriel, 'Assessing the "Humorous Temperament": Construction of the Facet and Standard Trait Forms of the State-Trait-Cheerfulness-Inventory – STCI.' *Humor: International Journal of Humor Research,* 1996, 9, 303–339. Used by permission.

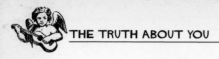

SCORING YOUR TEST

I have a delightful secret to share. These are my favourite sneaky type of tests that measure multiple traits about you. In addition to evaluating cheerfulness, these tests will also reveal information on your seriousness and ill humour. To score these quizzes, separate your answers into the three categories shown below. Write your scores from the previous pages in one column, your friend's results in the other.

For example, if you circled a '4' for question 1, write a '4' under Cheerfulness, question 1. The question numbers are separated into three tables. We will discuss your answers to all three sections.

CHEERFULNESS			SERIOUSNESS			BAD MOOD		
Quest. No.	Your Score	Friend's Score	Quest. No.	Your Score	Friend's Score	Quest. No.	Your Score	Friend's Score
1.	_____	_____	2.	_____	_____	3.	_____	_____
4.	_____	_____	5.	_____	_____	6.	_____	_____
7.	_____	_____	8.	_____	_____	9.	_____	_____
10.	_____	_____	11.	_____	_____	12.	_____	_____
13.	_____	_____	14.	_____	_____	15.	_____	_____
16.	_____	_____	17.	_____	_____	18.	_____	_____
19.	_____	_____	20.	_____	_____	21.	_____	_____
22.	_____	_____	23.	_____	_____	24.	_____	_____
25.	_____	_____	26.	_____	_____	27.	_____	_____
28.	_____	_____	29.	_____	_____	30.	_____	_____

Add Cheerfulness scores:

_____ _____

Add Seriousness scores:

_____ _____

Add Bad Mood scores:

_____ _____

UNDERSTANDING YOUR SCORE

We will look at your three scores separately. We start with your cheerful nature, then learn about your serious score and, finally, we'll visit the dark side to see how strong your bad moods are.

I added the friend's answer column next to yours so that you can easily compare yourself to your chum's opinions. The best way to gain insights from your friend's perspective is to read the analysis first with your scores, then look yourself up with your pal's scores. Don't worry about minor differences of a point or two between individual questions – focus on gaps of two points or more, and then compare the summaries of each trait. If your friend's perspective of you varies by more than ten points on cheerfulness, seriousness or bad mood, discuss these differences with your pal.

The score range of each category is 10 to 40. The higher your score on each category, the more cheerful, serious or ill-humoured you are.

YOUR CHEERFULNESS SCORE

YOUR SCORE	PERCENTILE	PERSONALITY
27 and less	15th	*Glum*
28 to 30	30th	*Gloomy*
31 to 34	50th	*Glad*
35 to 37	70th	*Glittering*
38 and higher	85th	*Gleeful*

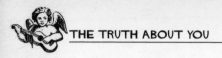

WHAT DOES YOUR SCORE MEAN?

30 or Less. Gloomy Gus.

Unfortunately, you can be a sourpuss who puts the lemon in lemonade. If you were among one hundred randomly picked people, lined up from most cheerful to least cheerful, you would be in the bottom third. Instead of letting the small problems of everyday life drift away, they accumulate in your mind and add up to misery. Reread the information in this chapter about the *happiness filter* and *unpleasant effect*. You have a blue filter that denies you some basic pleasure. Also, be sure to read the suggestions in chapter 7.

31 to 34. Glad Lad.

You are the cheerful sort. Your merry nature is about average. Your pleasant nature sees you through many of life's little peccadilloes, you smile frequently, and you enjoy a good laugh every now and then. You are happiest when surrounded by merrymakers. You enjoy having a good time, and your friends value your company. Read the suggestions for greater happiness in chapter 7.

35 and Higher. Miss Mary Sunshine!

My goodness, you are a merry soul. You freely share a laugh with friends, you probably have a beautiful smile from using it all the time and I bet you are a fun person to be with. Your friends may accuse you of seeing life through rose-coloured glasses, but what

the hell, you have the happiness filter on and you are enjoying it. You are in the top third for cheerfulness and (statistically at least) you will live longer than your gloomy peers.

YOUR SERIOUS SCORE

YOUR SCORE	PERCENTILE	PERSONALITY
20 and less	15th	*Sidesplitting*
21 to 22	30th	*Silly*
23 to 27	50th	*Sensible*
28 to 30	70th	*Solemn*
31 and higher	85th	*Sombre*

WHAT DOES YOUR SCORE MEAN?

22 or Less. Carefree and Cheery.
You have a light-hearted outlook on life, you prefer playing over work and in your book most of the world is far too serious. In fact, you are in the least serious third of the population. While you are fun at parties, some of your colleagues may grumble that you do not take life earnestly enough. Have fun, but don't overdo the silliness.

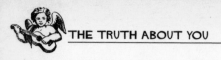

23 to 27. Thoughtful and Reflective.

A healthy balance between being too serious and too silly is your strong suit. You take life as it comes and distinguish foolishness from facts. People enjoy working with you as you can assess thoughtful ideas from fluff. Although you enjoy a bit of both, you can even them out and that makes you a fun, thoughtful friend. At work, you can be serious when necessary and then relax, release and have fun too. Your serious score is average, but don't despair – when it comes to this personality trait, average is excellent.

28 or More. Sombre and Solemn.

This book is not sober enough for you! You are in the top third for seriousness. As the author of this test, Dr Ruch, would say, you have 'the readiness to perceive, act, or communicate seriously'. Facts and objectivity are central to you, but often you do not realise that the most important things in life are the humorous moments that season each day. You may also live with situations that call for you to be more serious than you would like. Perhaps your colleagues at work expect you to be serious, or you are raising teenagers and believe sombre is the best parenting course. This is admirable, but try to see the humorous side of life while you are living it. Check out chapter 7 for more suggestions.

Your Bad Mood Score

YOUR SCORE	PERCENTILE	PERSONALITY
13 and less	15th	*Trippin'?*
14 to 16	30th	*Tranquil*
17 to 21	50th	*Tolerant*
22 to 24	70th	*Temperamental*
25 and higher	85th	*Tyrannical*

What Does Your Score Mean?

16 or Less. Blue Sky and Sunbeams.

Does nothing get you down? You laugh in the face of adversity. Singing in the rain comes naturally to you. When it comes to bad moods, you seldom have one; in fact, you are in the lowest third of the population for moodiness.

17 to 21. Shades of Grey.

Your responses to life's tribulations are rational and typical. You tend to be in good moods, but when upsetting things happen, you are rightfully affected by them. The moods you experience are about average. People know you as a good friend with a sense of humour and mental depth. Everyone can get crabby, but hey, you've got to have a good reason. See chapter 7 for ways to improve your moods.

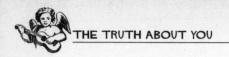

22 or More. The Dark Cloud.

You wake up on the wrong side of the bed most mornings. You can find a dark cloud on every silver lining. Sometimes you want to lighten up, but you struggle and it is tiring. You are often grumpy and in a bad mood. It's not your fault, you just don't feel like laughing often.

Review your satisfaction with life scores along with your cheerfulness and seriousness score. Many times we have to live with situations that can drain our happiness. There are ways to stop the flow. If your scores are gloomy on the other scales, it may be time to talk to a doctor about depression.

THE PEAK EXPERIENCES SCALE

So, now we have measured your general satisfaction with life and the individual elements that make you a happy or unhappy person (your cheerfulness, seriousness and bad moods), it is time for the icing on the cake: a measure of those supreme moments when life seems so perfect that time stands still. These are *peak experiences*.

Most of us occasionally experience simple, yet profound moments that make us appreciate how exquisite life is. These experiences can be big, like the birth of a child or a wedding day, but more frequently they are smaller, intimate moments like taking a walk and feeling at one with nature. You may be led to a peak expe-

rience by something as simple as a bird's song on a peaceful morning or the smell of the air after rain. It is that special sense of oneness with the universe and a greater appreciation of life that initiate peak experiences. You may have to think hard to realise that you have indeed experienced some peak moments.

You can't just make these experiences happen: they generally come about when all of your basic, primitive needs are met. Peak experiences come from nine sources of stimulation:

VENUES OF PEAK EXPERIENCES

Social	From interaction with others.
Artistic	From musical, visual or literary arts.
Athletic	Experiencing oneness with the game.
Nature	Primitive oneness with the universe.
Sexual	Feeling oneness from being with another.
Altruistic	A high from helping others.
Chemical	A high from a drug.
Academic	The thrill of learning.
Political	The thrill of putting your ideas into action.

TAKING THE TEST

Now that you have a better sense of what peak experiences are, let's get you measured. The original test is seventy questions long, so for

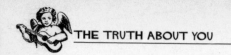

the sake of brevity, I have sampled forty questions to provide you with an approximate indicator of how the frequency of your peak experiences compares to others. If you are interested in the complete test, Dr Mathes's study is cited at the end of the quiz.

TEST YOURSELF

INSTRUCTIONS

The test you are about to take consists of forty questions. It only takes about ten to fifteen minutes to complete, but don't rush. There is no time limit. There are two columns of statements. Think about your experiences and circle **T** for true or **F** for false, as appropriate.

THE PEAK EXPERIENCES TEST

The following statements describe a variety of experiences. Read each statement carefully, then indicate if it is true or false for you. There are two columns, each with its own stem sentence. The first column consists of experiences you may have had; the second column lists experiences you may never have had.

I have had an experience that made me extremely happy and, at least temporarily, . . .

I have *never* had an experience that made me extremely happy and, at least temporarily, . . .

---

1. Made me feel more unique than I usually feel.   T   F

2. Removed much of my perplexity and confusion.   T   F

---

3. Caused me to feel that the world was sacred.   T   F

4. Moved me closer to a perfect identity.   T   F

---

5. Caused my private, selfish concerns to fade away.   T   F

6. Helped me to totally accept the world.   T   F

---

7. Gave my whole life new meaning.   T   F

8. Made me want to do something good for the world.   T   F

---

9. Caused time to seem to stand still.   T   F

10. Made me feel very lucky and fortunate.   T   F

---

11. Caused me to feel great kindness toward humanity.   T   F

12. Made me feel as if all my wants and needs were satisfied.   T   F

---

13. Caused me to like and accept everyone.   T   F

14. Allowed me to realise that everyone has his/her place in the universe.   T   F

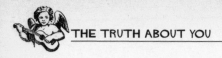

I have had an experience that made me extremely happy and, at least temporarily, . . .

I have *never* had an experience that made me extremely happy and, at least temporarily, . . .

15. Caused me to feel that the world is totally good.　**T F**

16. Made me more accepting of pain than I usually am.　**T F**

17. Caused me to become disoriented in time.　**T F**

18. Made me feel both proud and humble at the same time.　**T F**

19. Removed many of my inhibitions.　**T F**

20. Gave me a sense of obligation to do constructive things.　**T F**

21. Made me feel freer than I usually feel.　**T F**

22. Involved total listening.　**T F**

23. Made me very grateful for the privilege of having had it.　**T F**

24. Gave my life new worth.　**T F**

25. Made me feel as if I had everything. I could not think of anything else that I wanted.　**T F**

26. Caused me to feel that the world is totally beautiful.　**T F**

I have had an experience that made me extremely happy and, at least temporarily, . . .

I have *never* had an experience that made me extremely happy and, at least temporarily, . . .

27. Reduced my anxiety level greatly.   **T F**

28. Helped me to appreciate beauty to a greater degree than I usually do.   **T F**

29. Caused me to believe that I could not be disappointed by anyone.   **T F**

30. Put me in a state of total concentration.   **T F**

31. Gave me great insight.   **T F**

32. Led me to realise that there is a meaningfulness to the universe.   **T F**

33. Caused me to feel that people are sacred.   **T F**

34. Caused me to view the world as totally desirable.   **T F**

35. Led me to accept everything.   **T F**

36. Made the conflicts of life seem to disappear.   **T F**

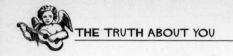

I have had an experience that made me extremely happy and, at least temporarily, ...	I have *never* had an experience that made me extremely happy and, at least temporarily, ...
37. Caused me to become disoriented in space. T F	**38.** Helped me to a greater appreciation of perfection. T F
39. Helped me to realise that I could never commit suicide. T F	**40.** Led me to believe that I could die with dignity. T F

END OF TEST

Used with permission of Dr Eugene W. Mathes, Western Illinois University. For further information, see E.W. Mathes, et al., 'Peak Experience Tendencies: Scale Development and Theory Testing'. *Journal of Humanistic Psychology,* 1982, 22, 92–108.

SCORING YOUR TEST

Scoring this test is very simple: Give yourself one point for each of
your answers that match the answer key.

PEAK EXPERIENCES ANSWER KEY

1. T	9. T	17. T	25. T	33. T
2. F	10. F	18. F	26. F	34. F
3. T	11. T	19. T	27. T	35. T
4. F	12. F	20. F	28. F	36. F
5. T	13. T	21. T	29. T	37. T
6. F	14. F	22. F	30. F	38. F
7. T	15. T	23. T	31. T	39. T
8. F	16. F	24. F	32. F	40. F

Number correct: _____

YOUR SCORE: WOMEN	YOUR SCORE: MEN	PERCENTILE
23 and less	22 and less	15th
24 to 27	23 to 26	30th
28 to 32	27 to 31	50th
33 to 35	32 to 34	70th
36 and higher	35 and higher	85th

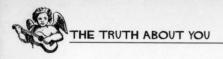

WHAT DOES YOUR SCORE MEAN?

Women tend to report slightly more peak experiences than men, so to adjust for this, the scoring is a little different for either sex.

Women: 27 or Less. Men: 26 or Less. Nose to the Grindstone.
Unfortunately, you seldom have peak experiences. You are in the bottom third of the population when it comes to enjoying peak experiences. You tend to focus to on the concrete tasks of the day and do not stop to smell the roses. This does not mean that you can't have peak experiences, but you do not open yourself up to self-discovery. Given the chance to be less practical and more reflective, you could enjoy more of these intensely happy times.

Women: 28 to 32. Men: 27 to 31. Feet Flat on the Ground.
You experience these moments of extreme happiness with a frequency that is about average. You tend to maintain a healthy balance between asserting your mental needs and being self-sufficient with the need to conform and follow the rules of others. You have a pragmatic, practical side, but it is well balanced with your imaginative, experimental side. You have the tools to enjoy life well.

Women: 33 or More. Men: 32 or More. Head in the Clouds.
You are a creative, astute visionary. You tend to be tolerant and understanding, yet assertive and expedient when necessary. You

have confidence in yourself, both publicly and privately, and you are in touch with the sensual side of your life. Perhaps you even achieve Zen-like trances of oneness when you do tasks you really enjoy. When it comes to frequency of peak experiences, you are in the top third of the population.

How Do You Compare?

Now that you know how happy you are, think about how your results compare to these studies of happiness. We'll begin with large studies of entire countries and societies, followed by those of individuals like you.

HOW HAPPY IS EVERYBODY ELSE?

Pretty darn happy, really. While the nightly news might make you think life is miserable, when people are asked to rate their lives, they are generally happy. In 1960, almost 90 per cent of Americans considered themselves either 'pretty happy' or 'very happy'. That level of subjective well-being has been fairly constant up to today.

However, it is not just Americans who are happy. Psychologists Ed and Carol Diener from the University of Illinois reviewed happiness data in forty-three countries and found that the people in almost 90 per cent of countries surveyed had a positive subjective well-being. While there are plenty of happy people in Canada,

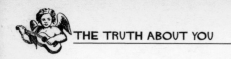

Europe and Scandinavia, happiness is not solely a Western phenomenon. Some of the happiest countries include Brazil, Japan and Thailand. Meanwhile, people from India and the Dominican Republic reported being least happy.

ARE PEOPLE IN WEALTHY COUNTRIES HAPPIER?

Yes and no. There is some correlation between gross national product per capita and the average happiness of a nation, but there are plenty of disparities. Scandinavians and Australians are a happy lot. Year after year, they are more satisfied with life than the rest of us. But they have less money than their wealthier North American cousins. The per person gross national product in the United States is about three times that of the average Irish citizen. Yet the Irish are consistently more satisfied with their lives than Americans.

WHAT IS YOUR HAPPY LIFE EXPECTANCY?

Dutch social psychologist Ruut Veenhoven developed a clever measurement called Happy Life Expectancy. Basically, it is the average life expectancy for each country multiplied by the overall happiness rating of its citizens. For example, the average American lives for seventy-six years. Coincidentally, studies indicate that people in the United States are happy 76 per cent of the time. By multiplying these numbers, Veenhoven reckons that the average American can expect to have 57.8 happy years over his or her life. The table opposite gives a general idea of where you can live to find the most happiness.

ESTIMATED NUMBER OF HAPPY YEARS
IN SELECTED COUNTRIES

COUNTRY	LIFE EXPECTANCY YEARS	HAPPY YEARS
Iceland	78	62.0
Netherlands	77	61.7
Sweden	78	61.5
Australia	78	59.5
Ireland	75	59.2
Britain	76	57.9
United States	76	57.8
Northern Ireland	74	56.5
France	77	55.4
New Zealand	76	54.9
Japan	80	53.0
Canada	77	52.9
Spain	78	52.8
Germany	76	51.7
Mexico	71	46.0
Brazil	66	42.9
South Africa	63	38.2
India	60	36.4

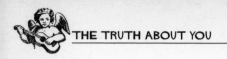

WOULD YOU LIKE TO LIVE TO 100?

As more and more people are reaching the elusive 100 mark, we have learned some interesting facts about centenarians. It seems that by the time we are 60, we will have picked up pretty much every chronic disease of aging we are going to get. The risk of getting these diseases actually goes *down* once we hit 80 years and beyond. The best way to live to be 100 is to . . . you guessed it! Be happy! While a healthy lifestyle will help you live longer, so will a good sense of humour. Incidentally, the other traits of those with long lives include: being conscientious, being dependable, working hard, managing stress and not being quick to anger.

CAN MONEY BUY YOU HAPPINESS?

Yes and no. Yes, sufficient money to put clothes on your back and bread on the table does bring happiness. However, once our basic needs for food, shelter and human contact are met, additional money soon has a negligible effect. How many times have you dreamed of the fun you would have buying things when you won the lottery? Or have you thought to yourself just how much happier you would be with a 10 per cent raise? It turns out that you would probably be no more happy than you are today.

One surprising fact from research in this area suggests that our income does not matter nearly as much as how satisfied we are with it. Even if you don't have much, if you are content with your income, you are bound to be happier than wealthy folks who

always want 'more'. Acceptance is a stepping-stone on the path to greater happiness.

Now, if money *could* buy happiness, how much would people pay? According to a 1997 poll by *USA Today,* when some of the wealthiest Americans were asked how much they would pay for certain privileges, they learned that the wealthy would pay just over four hundred thousand dollars for great intellect, almost five hundred thousand dollars for true love and six hundred and forty thousand dollars for a place in heaven.

WHEN IS THE HAPPIEST TIME OF YOUR LIFE?

At what stage in our lives are we happiest? Is it during our carefree teenage salad days? As a young adult with new freedoms? While experiencing the joys of raising children in adulthood? Or are we happiest once the children leave home and we can enjoy our golden years in peace?

Generally speaking, happiness increases over the years. But if you get married, the pattern is a little different. Sociologist Terri Orbuch and her colleagues from the University of Michigan found that marital happiness tends to increase during the first few years of marriage and then declines for the next ten to twenty years! The good news is that after twenty years, the level of marital happiness increases to levels beyond the honeymoon phase. Why? It seems that the pitter-patter of little feet places a strain on domestic bliss. It is only once the children are out of the house that wedded bliss can

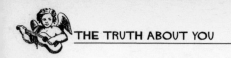

continue to grow. Orbuch also found that couples are most likely to consider divorce after fifteen to nineteen years of marriage.

Furthermore, a 2003 study in the *Journal of Marriage and Family* finds that the wealthiest couples endure the biggest drop in happiness once they have children. It seems that more affluent couples have more to miss; they lament their carefree travel days with plenty of recreational and social activities. In contrast, the lifestyle changes a baby brings to middle-class and low-income couples are not so extensive. So, if you can stay the course and make it over those crucial years, thoughts of divorce may fade away. Greatest happiness correlates with the times in our lives when the children leave the nest and we retire.

INITIAL IMPRESSIONS

Did you know that your initials can help you live longer?

A psychologist at the University of California found that people who have positive monograms such as JOY, WOW and ACE live longer that those whose initials spell APE, DUD, ILL or PIG.

It seems that if your initials spell out something negative like RAT, people mention it from time to time through your life, from grade school to old age. The theory is that each time you are teased or mocked, a few minutes are shaved off your life. Conversely, you get a little boost whenever someone mentions your initials in a positive light. These little boosts can add years to your life.

IS LAUGHTER REALLY THE BEST MEDICINE?

Yes, it is – at least in small doses. While many studies indicate that negative, stressful experiences can make us ill, psychiatrist Kathleen Dillon and her colleagues had a great idea for a study of how happiness may help keep us well. Students were asked to spit into test tubes before and after watching a humorous and a neutral videotape. Their spit was then analysed to see how much immunoglobulin A (an immune system chemical that defends the body against viruses) it contained. Sure enough, watching the funny video increased the body's immune defences. Although the boost from the video faded within minutes, people who use humour to cope with life's problems do maintain higher levels of immunity.

Two Yale psychologists also took a broad look at the effect of happiness on health. In a series of experiments they found that sad people suffering from the common cold complained more of aches and pains than their happier counterparts. Sad sufferers also felt less able to help themselves get better; they wallowed in their illness. Happier sufferers were more likely to help themselves improve. Further, happy people believed they were less likely to get sick in the future.

BEHIND THE LAUGHTER AND THE TEARS:

- Women cry four times more often than men.

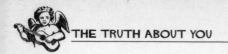

- A good laugh lowers blood pressure. Holding back tears increases blood pressure.

- About 85 per cent of women and 75 per cent of men feel better after a good cry.

- Tears are powerful signals; they shout something is wrong! We are wired to become kinder and less aggressive when we see them. A few drops on the cheeks can turn an aggressor into an ally.

- Expressing emotions enables self-disclosure. Sometimes we are uncertain of our emotions until we hear ourselves laugh or see our tears.

DO YOU SEE HAPPINESS?

A group of researchers from Virginia set out to determine if our brains were specifically wired to recognise happiness. The researchers asked healthy men and women to look into a special box called a tachistoscope, which psychologists use to quickly flash images. Then, pictures of either happy, angry or neutral faces were flashed one at a time into the eyes of each participant. The participants were asked to press one of two buttons labelled as 'happy' and 'angry' as quickly as possible. The results are interesting:

- Men and women see happiness more quickly than anger. This

may be because our brains are wired to detect happy emotions or we anticipate happiness when we see faces.

- Men were faster at detecting the happy faces. This is because men have one well-developed happiness detector in the right side of their brain. The right side of the brain is thought to play a larger role in visual tasks.

- Women have happiness detectors on both sides of their brains, but they are not as well developed. Men tend to use one side of the brain or the other, whereas women integrate information using both sides of the brain. So women can detect happy faces; it just takes a little longer since both sides of the brain need to agree.

HOW DO YOU HEAR HAPPINESS?

Dr Philip Bryden and his associates at the University of Waterloo in Canada conducted a similar experiment to the one above. Dr Bryden played happy, sad, angry and neutral voices into earphones worn by healthy college students. Their results? People could detect happy voices more accurately than sad, angry or neutral.

CAN YOU SMELL HAPPINESS?

People who are happy tend to remember happy events. Likewise, those who are sad tend to recall upsetting events. In a study funded by the Fragrance Research Fund, Howard Ehrlichman and Jack

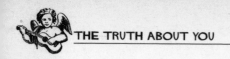

Halpern studied how odour can affect which memories we recall.

For this experiment, the researchers gave over one hundred women a sniff of either a pleasant-smelling almond extract or a malodorous solution of pyridine. The volunteers were then asked to remember some of their real life events and then rate how happy the memory was. Sure enough, the pleasant odour elicited more pleasant memories, while the unpleasant odour led to unhappy memories. How this mechanism works is not clear, but it may be that a pleasant smell makes us feel happy and therefore makes it easier to retrieve happy memories.

REEKING RESEARCH

Smell is a great thing to study. Just think about it; smells have four marvellous attributes:

1. Odours are salient: they are either pleasant or unpleasant, and there is little middle ground for study participants to get confused.
2. Odours are easy to control in the laboratory.
3. Your study participants need few brain cells: virtually no mental effort is required to experience a smell.
4. Odours seem to affect the brain directly without much competition from other stimuli.

So, if you are considering a career in research, you may want to start by picking noses.

DO YOU HAVE A GOOD MEMORY?
Now that we have seen that being happy leads to retrieving happy events, let's look at the effect of happiness on making new memories. Two psychologists from Louisiana made fifty college students happy, sad or neutral by asking them to read cheery, gloomy or dispassionate stories. They then gave the students sixteen words to remember. Twenty minutes later the students again read the 'mood-induction' passages. Finally, they were asked to recall as many of the sixteen words as possible. The results were clear: happy people learned more, and those who were happy during both learning and recall parts of the study were able to remember the most words.

ARE YOU GALLANT?
Does mood affect compliance? Psychologists believe that if you are in a good mood and someone asks you to do something, you are likely to view the requestor as truly in need of help. The favour seems reasonable. Conversely, the theory suggests, when you are angry you perceive a requestor as being manipulative and the request as biased. Drs Sandra Milberg and Margaret Clark conducted an experiment that found the happier the subjects, the more likely they were to acquiesce to the wishes of another. Their results also suggest an interesting enigma: although sad people are less likely to help another, it is

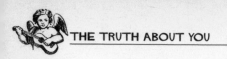

they who can most benefit by becoming happier as they do good deeds. As a result, sad people tend to stay sad and happy people increase their well-being by helping others.

In another study, Alice Isen and Paul Levin set out to make us a little happier, to see if we would be more willing to help. Alice and Paul staked out a library. One of them randomly gave biscuits to some of the people who visited the library. Later, in a seemingly unrelated encounter, the other researcher asked the person for help on a task. You guessed it, the people who got a biscuit were more willing to help out.

The experimenters then tried to replicate their findings by leaving coins in public telephone booths. Some unwitting telephone users got a little profit while others found nothing. Shortly after either finding the coins or finding nothing, the subjects saw someone who had dropped a stack of papers. It turns out that significantly more of those who found the coins helped pick up the papers. These studies support the premise of 'random acts of kindness'. If you can do something to make someone's day a little brighter, your generosity will pay dividends.

ARE YOU JUDGEMENTAL?

An Australian and an American psychologist gave fifty college students a personality test. After the test, half of the students were told they did wonderfully on the test and that they had excellent personalities. The other half were met with frowns and comments

like 'bad' and 'this is terrible' and were told they had problematic personalities. Unbeknownst to the students, they were not really having their papers graded, they were having their moods manipulated. They were tricked into feeling happy or sad.

Then the students were asked to read about four different people and judge whether they were likeable, competent, happy, likely to be good workers, etc. They found that people who were happy made positive judgements more quickly and spent little time reading negative details. The sad students seemed to dwell on the negative details of the people they were judging. Finally, when asked to remember the descriptions, happy people remembered more positive details.

CAN THE WEATHER MAKE YOU ANGRY?

'How the hell should I know!' That may be the response you'd expect on a hot day. A trio of researchers from the University of Missouri found that hot weather can make us both angry and excited. But worst of all, we don't realise how irritable the heat is making us. The study found that our anger increases steadily from a low level when the temperature is in the low seventies Fahrenheit and increases as the mercury reaches the nineties. Unfortunately, in the heat of the moment we don't realise what is happening. Remember the excitation transfer theory we learned about in Chapter 3 (see page 109). The same theory applies here. We mistakenly attribute our anger to the behaviour of others.

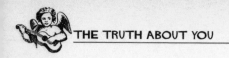

ARE YOUR REGRETS MAKING YOU SAD?

We all have some regrets in life. Maybe you regret never asking out that special boy or girl in class. Or maybe you once said something you should not have. We have two kinds of regrets in life: regrets for the things we did but wish we hadn't and regrets for the things we didn't do but wish we had. Interestingly, it is what we did *not* do that truly haunts us. The *Washington Post* interviewed over one thousand U.S. adults and found that over 60 per cent of respondents regretted missing out on certain experiences. Only 21 per cent regretted doing some things they had done and a lucky 12 per cent reported no regrets at all.

DO YOU FEEL DEPRESSED DURING THE WINTER?

Seasonal affective disorder (SAD) is a clinical name for winter depression, a condition brought on by light deprivation. The symptoms include overeating, oversleeping and craving carbohydrates. Women tend to be slightly more prone to SAD than men. Also, it seems that people who are narcissistic suffer more from SAD. Estimates are that about 10 per cent of Finns are susceptible to some SAD effects and 5 per cent of American adults seek medical help due to SAD.

The cure is exposure to bright light. In fact, there are 'light cafés' in Scandinavia where one can enjoy a good shine in the face. However, it appears that a gentle increase in light intensity, such as one that mimics dawn, is the best prescription. It is speculated that

a good dose of light in the morning decreases the production of melatonin, which is thought to be responsible for the winter blues.

If you don't like bright light shining in your face, don't despair. The light does not have to shine in your eyes. Researchers Scot Campbell and Patricia Murphy shone light on the backs of people's knees and achieved similar success. Why? The researchers speculate that it is our blood rather than the eyes that registers the amount of light the body receives. Haemoglobin (the red stuff in blood) is very similar to chlorophyll (the green stuff in plants). Haemoglobin may work in the body like chlorophyll works in plants, telling us when it is day and night.

One of the most interesting aspects of this research is its implications. Think of the effects of small kneepad-like straps containing little optical lights and a timer. Those with SAD could strap them on at night and get a good extra dose of light an hour before the alarm goes off.

Unfortunately, if you don't suffer from winter depression, there is always *summer* depression. That's right. People living nearer the equator have a greater chance of getting this condition attributed to higher temperatures.

DO YOU KNOW THE SECRETS TO HAPPINESS?

*Most folks are about as happy as they
make up their minds to be.* ABRAHAM LINCOLN

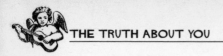

Abraham Lincoln had it just about right, and this next experiment should help you keep his wisdom in mind. Psychologists Jennifer Crocker and Lisa Gallo found that after completing this sentence five times people felt much better about their lives:

Complete this sentence five times:

1. *I'm glad I am not a* _____

2. *I'm glad I am not a* _____

3. *I'm glad I am not a* _____

4. *I'm glad I am not a* _____

5. *I'm glad I am not a* _____

THE PATH TO GREATER HAPPINESS

- Accept yourself as who you are; seek growth, not perfection.

- Accept responsibility for your actions; take control of your life.

- Eat well, exercise and stimulate your mind with new activities.

- Enjoy the simple things in life.

- Foster friendships, listen more and talk less. Be kind to strangers.

- Set some realistic goals in life and go for them.

- Live for today. Don't worry about tomorrow; it can take care of itself.

- Forgive others; don't criticise them.

- Put whatever guilt, anger, hate and selfishness you are carrying around in a box and throw it out. None of us can go back in time to fix the past.

- Don't expect all your dreams to come true. Pick one or two and work at them.

- Let's not overanalyse it, because whatever happiness is, be grateful that you are still around to enjoy it.

- Turn off the television and get a good night's sleep.

6

MOTIVATION AND CONTROL

The harder I work, the luckier I get. SAMUEL GOLDWYN

Have you noticed that, after succeeding on a difficult task, some people say, 'I tried, and tried, and I finally did it', while others remark, 'I guess I was just at the right place at the right time'? When things are going well, are you the type of person who says, 'Touch wood', and gives a couple of gentle taps to the nearest table or door? Or do you report that things are going well because you are making them work? Success in life is attributed to either luck or personal effort. Your belief affects your behaviour and the way you see the world.

Psychologists call this characteristic *locus of control*. Like any good personality trait, locus of control has been carefully studied by psychologists – with many interesting results. Locus of control is intriguing because it affects so many different aspects of our lives. At the end of this chapter I will describe the results of various studies that explore the fascinating things we do because of our locus of control beliefs. But first, let's learn a little more about locus of control.

WHAT IS LOCUS OF CONTROL?

Many of life's experiences are considered to be good, bad or some-where in between. Locus of control is also like this: it is a continuum. You can believe that your accomplishments in life are due to luck, or personal effort, or somewhere in between. Psychologists call people who take the credit for success and the blame for failure 'internals'. Internals believe they are responsible for the good and bad things that happen to them. Internals tend to be self-reliant; they take pride in victory and they feel shame in defeat. 'Externals', on the other hand, blame outside forces or bad luck for their failures and attribute their successes to good fortune. Extreme externals do not believe their behaviour has any effect on their lot in life. Externals are fatalistic. In short, internals do things and externals have things done to them. Of course, many people fall in the middle of this continuum. Individuals who maintain a balance between internalism and externalism are often happier. They know what is within their control and what is not.

The concept of locus of control has deep cultural and social implications. Why? Because it influences motivation. When you plan to do something, you consider the effects of your behaviour. For example, you may want to get paid more at work. If you are an internal (you believe you control your destiny), you will work harder to get that payrise. However, if you are an external (you believe your efforts will not influence your destiny), to you harder work will not be rewarded. But if you are lucky, you'll get a rise.

Locus of control has been described as the best kept secret in psychology. It has been studied in depth for over thirty years, yet few non-psychologists know about it. This chapter will let you in on the secret; you will explore how your locus of control affects you. Use this chapter wisely, and you will better understand yourself and others.

INTERNAL PERSONALITIES

Thomas Edison embodies the internal personality. He is best known for characterising his success as '. . . 99 per cent perspiration and 1 per cent inspiration'. Edison's work style was tenacious. He surrounded himself with bright, creative people and worked them hard. When looking for the right filament for his light, he tried carbonised platinum, nickel, coconut shell, fishing line, human hair, macaroni, onion rind and then six thousand types of bamboo sent to him from all over the world. In 1932, Edison told *Harper's Magazine*: 'The trouble with inventors is that they try a few things and quit. I never quit until I get what I want!'

Edison trusted nothing to luck or good fortune. Although repeatedly referred to as 'The Wizard' in the press, he had no time for the supernatural or superstitions. An ardent agnostic throughout his eighty-one years, Edison believed that in order to make things work, he needed to be in control.

EXTERNAL PERSONALITIES

In the United States, they tend to respect those who have pulled themselves up by their bootstraps and overcome obstacles using their own ingenuity and get-up-and-go. Successful American externals are difficult to find. We occasionally hear about people who live their lives in anonymity, buy a lottery ticket and happen to win millions of dollars, but Americans tend to discount the efforts of those whose lives have changed due to luck. And although some may admire the cloistered nuns and monks who place their lives in the hands of God, it is the internals we revere.

A Brief History of
Locus of Control Testing

In the mid-1950s, a twenty-three-year-old Korean War veteran was sent to psychologist Julian Rotter for mental health therapy. After repeated visits from the patient, it dawned on Rotter that the veteran was not responding to treatment because he saw no link between his behaviour and rewards. The patient felt that he had absolutely no control over his life. This unusual mind-set could not be explained by current concepts in psychology of the day. Because the veteran did not respond to opportunities to get rewards, his behaviour did not fit the mechanistic 'behaviourism' theories that were dominant in the 1950s. Thus, Rotter developed the concept of locus of control to help explain this tendency. His ideas came in the early 1960s, a time when the field of psychology and American society were ready for change.

The 1960s were turbulent times. During this period, nonconformity and a philosophy of questioning authority became intensely popular, partially in response to the Vietnam War. Behaviouristic principles could no longer explain the full range of human behaviour. The field of psychology began research into cognitive functions (like language, memory and thinking). Rotter attempted to bridge the gap between the old and the new with his work in social learning theory.

Dr Rotter's theories were akin to pouring petrol on the wildfire of psychological change. The revolutionary ideas of social-learning theory have permeated and evolved through psychology for the past forty years. Dr Rotter's work led to a rush of fascinating research. By 1966, a leading scientist in the field of locus of control, Herbert Lefcourt, guessed that '. . . groups whose social position is one of minimal power either by class or race tend to score higher in the external direction'. Lefcourt had it right.

African Americans. African Americans tend to be more external than European Americans, even after variables like social and economic status are taken into account. However, African Americans may tend to be external because externalism is reality for this group. It is possible that black Americans are currently unable to exert the same control over their lives as white Americans. African Americans may be more realistic because reality for this group means less personal control.

U.S. Hispanics. Generally, adult Hispanic Americans are less internal than adult, white, non-Hispanic Americans. However, education plays a part; several studies failed to find any locus of control differences between Hispanic Americans and European Americans at the high school or college level. In fact, Garza and Ames found that Mexican American college students were significantly more internal after factors like gender and social and economic status were removed.

Women. One fact that has been found in many countries is that women are generally more external than men. Numerous studies show that women are less internal, although cultural trends are still apparent. For example, Japanese women are even more external than American women.

The feminist revolution in American thinking between the 1950s and 1980s was profound. Young people, women and minority groups made significant gains in civil rights. Women in particular made advances to achieve previously unheard-of control over their own lives. Women in the United States made gains in employment and created a national campaign to pass the Equal Rights Amendment. Do you think greater personal control shifted the American woman's locus of control? *Wrong!* Surprisingly, there has been virtually no change in female locus of control throughout the women's movement. The expected shift to internalism has not appeared. It seems that the social progress U.S. women made is still not sufficient to change locus of control psychology on a national level. We must question whether American women have made sufficient social and political gains to believe they are in complete control of their lives.

Okay, enough of history and sociology. It is time to measure you.

TEST YOURSELF

Your locus of control influences your behaviour tremendously. Your belief has deep roots in many areas of everyday life. The following test was developed by Dr Julian Rotter and then shortened and improved by Dr Hanna Levenson. Take the test and then we will discuss your score. Most people who take this test do so without knowing what it measures. Do not try to second-guess any answers or worry about the desirability of your score. Answer each question truthfully.

INSTRUCTIONS

Please answer the following questions by circling any number from one to five after each statement. One means you strongly disagree with the statement and five means you strongly agree with the statement. Circle one number next to each of the twenty-four statements listed on the test. There are no right or wrong answers, and there is no time limit.

LOCUS OF CONTROL TEST

For each statement, please use the following five-point scale where 1 means you strongly disagree with the statement and 5 means you strongly agree with the statement.

1. Whether or not I get to be a leader depends mostly on my ability.

Strongly Disagree				Strongly Agree
1	**2**	**3**	**4**	**5**

2. To a great extent my life is controlled by accidental happenings.

Strongly Disagree   Strongly Agree

      1   2   3   4   5

3. I feel that what happens in my life is mostly determined by powerful people.

             1   2   3   4   5

4. Whether or not I get into a car accident depends mostly on how good a driver I am.

             1   2   3   4   5

5. When I make plans, I am almost certain to make them work.

      1   2   3   4   5

6. Often there is no chance of protecting my personal interest from bad luck happening.

             1   2   3   4   5

7. When I get what I want, it's usually because I'm lucky.

      1   2   3   4   5

8. Although I might have good ability I will not be given leadership responsibility without appealing to those in positions of power.

             1   2   3   4   5

9. How many friends I have depends on how nice a person I am.

Strongly Disagree				Strongly Agree
1	2	3	4	5

10. I have often found that what is going to happen will happen.

1	2	3	4	5

11. My life is chiefly controlled by powerful others.

1	2	3	4	5

12. Whether I get into a car accident is mostly a matter of luck.

1	2	3	4	5

13. People like myself have very little chance of protecting our personal interests when they conflict with those of strong pressure groups.

1	2	3	4	5

14. It's not always wise for me to plan too far ahead because many things turn out to be a matter of good or bad fortune.

1	2	3	4	5

15. Getting what I want requires pleasing those people above me.

1	2	3	4	5

16. Whether or not I get to be a leader depends on whether I'm lucky enough to be in the right place at the right time.

| Strongly Disagree | | | | Strongly Agree |
| 1 | 2 | 3 | 4 | 5 |

17. If important people were to decide they didn't like me, I probably wouldn't make many friends.

| 1 | 2 | 3 | 4 | 5 |

18. I can pretty much determine what will happen in my life.

| 1 | 2 | 3 | 4 | 5 |

19. I am usually able to protect my personal interests.

| 1 | 2 | 3 | 4 | 5 |

20. Whether or not I get into a car accident depends mostly on the other driver.

| 1 | 2 | 3 | 4 | 5 |

21. When I get what I want, it's usually because I worked hard for it.

| 1 | 2 | 3 | 4 | 5 |

22. In order to have my plans work, I make sure that they fit in with the desires of people who have power over me.

| 1 | 2 | 3 | 4 | 5 |

23. My life is determined by my own actions.

Strongly Disagree				**Strongly Agree**
1	**2**	**3**	**4**	**5**

24. It's chiefly a matter of fate whether or not I have a few friends or many friends.

1	**2**	**3**	**4**	**5**

END OF TEST

Hanna Levenson, 'Distinctions Within the Concept of Internal-External Control:

Development of a New Scale', Paper Presented at the American Psychological Association,

1972. Used by permission.

SCORING YOUR TEST

Hidden in the test you have just taken are three different measurements – *internal/external, chance* and *power*. Separate your answers into the three categories shown as three tables below. We will discuss your answers to all three sections. Enter the numbers you circled on the previous pages on the tables opposite.

For example, if you circled a '4' for question 1, write a '4' under Internal/External, question 1. Note: The question numbers are separated into the three tables.

INTERNAL/EXTERNAL		CHANCE		POWER	
Question No.	Your Score	Question No.	Your Score	Question No.	Your Score
1.	_____	2.	_____	3.	_____
4.	_____	6.	_____	8.	_____
5.	_____	7.	_____	11.	_____
9.	_____	10.	_____	13.	_____
18.	_____	12.	_____	15.	_____
19.	_____	14.	_____	17.	_____
21.	_____	16.	_____	20.	_____
23.	_____	24.	_____	22.	_____
Add Internal/External scores:	_____	**Add Chance scores:**	_____	**Add Power scores:**	_____

UNDERSTANDING YOUR SCORE

We will look at your three scores separately. We will start with the internal/external continuum, then learn about your belief in chance. Finally, we will see how much power you believe you have over your life.

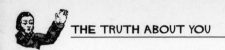

YOUR INTERNAL/EXTERNAL SCORE

Score of 8 to 21. External.

You are an *external*. You tend to feel that you do not control many aspects of your life. You believe that many things in life happen because of either good or bad luck or being in the right place at the right time. You tend to accept life's victories and defeats as they come. You are more fatalistic than higher scorers and may feel a sense of helplessness in your day-to-day life. You believe that when bad things happen, they are often unavoidable, and they occur simply due to bad luck or the mistakes of others. You may feel that you were born a certain way and that you cannot change.

You tend to get along well with people; you are more outgoing and friendly than internals. You may actually be more of a realist than the internals. If you are a woman or from a disadvantaged minority group, your external disposition may be based more on reality than superstition. You may feel that you have less control over your options in life because that is, in fact, the case. As you read the studies listed at the end of this chapter, think about what you can do to encourage or prevent the situations outlined.

Extra low scorers: If you scored between 8 and 12, you need to learn to take more responsibility for your actions. You can make a difference and you do count. Discover the ways in which your actions affect others. Learn to realise that your behaviour has meaning. If you are seriously superstitious or feel helpless much of the time, you may be prone to anxiety, depression and poor health. Review some of your answers on the test and think about whether these items are actually under your control.

Score of 22 to 30. Balanced.

Your score is in the mid-range. You have a balanced perspective of what is within your control and what is not. This test was devised to measure a general level of locus of control, and you are a complex person who leans towards internalism in some circumstances and externalism in others. For example, at work you may believe that much of what you do is under the control of others (external), but once you get home your activities are under your control (internal). Or you may believe that you do not have as much control as you would like over your relationships, but you can exert greater personal control over your leisure time.

You may have learned to view your level of control from your experiences in specific situations. For example, people who tend to be internal but who have severe health problems may learn to accept the fact that they do not retain control over their health. As you compare yourself with the others in the studies listed at the end of this chapter, think about how you would react to the situations described. In some circumstances you may be internal, and in others you may be external.

Score of 31 to 40. Internal.

You are an *internal*. You tend to take the initiative and go for the things you want in life. You are reliable. You hold yourself accountable for your actions and believe that your accomplishments in life are due to your efforts. You tend to be harder on yourself when life's disappointments strike. When things do not turn out the way they should, you take the blame. You prefer to play games where you can test or show off your skill. You get things done by focusing your energy on them; getting the job done means more to you than dealing with social niceties. You cherish your independence. You do not like to be in situations where others must take control: for example, if you become ill, you dislike relying on others to care for you.

Extra high scorers: If your score is 37 to 40, try to lighten up. You are not responsible for hurricanes and earthquakes. Sometimes things in life happen without your intervention. You are probably better off working alone. If you work with others, try to ease up on them; consider their feelings and be kinder to them. A word of caution: although you take great personal pride in your victories, you also feel greater shame in failure. Review some of your answers on the test and think about whether these items are actually under your control.

YOUR CHANCE SCORE

Now that you know whether you are an internal, an external, or someone in the middle range, this next set of answers will clarify your beliefs in the effect of chance in your life.

Score of 8 to 16. Sceptic.

You do not believe that your life is strongly influenced by chance and happenstance. You tend to believe that the world is an ordered place and that there are reasons that explain even unusual occurrences. You believe your actions and the actions of others control your destiny, rather than haphazard, random circumstances. You may play the lottery or games of chance, but you do so for enjoyment rather than to make money. If you are an internal, you strongly believe that your actions determine your destiny. If you are an external, you probably believe that you have little opportunity to control your own life and that your fate is determined by others.

Extra low scorers: If you scored 8 to 10, you tend to overanalyse situations. Sometimes unexplained occurrences happen and sometimes you are successful due to pure luck. Review the questions and see if some items listed are actually better described as chance.

Score of 17 to 26. Realist.

Your score is in the mid-range. You have a balanced perspective of what people can control and what they cannot. You know that when problems arise, they are sometimes the result of people's mistakes, and sometimes they are the random results of our unexplained world.

Score of 27 to 40. True believer.

You are a great believer in chance. You see life as a game of chance rather than a game of skill. You often believe that when unplanned things happen to you, they are due to fortune rather than your behaviour or the efforts of others. If you are an external, you feel that luck or destiny control your life rather than the actions of others. If you are an internal, you view yourself as a 'lucky gambler' who sees a chance and goes for it.

Extra high scorers: If you scored 37 to 40, you believe too much in chance. Your behaviour and the actions of others do make a difference. Go back and look at your 'chance' answers; think about how your behaviour may affect some of these situations.

YOUR POWER SCORE

Now that you know how internal or external you are and how much you believe in chance, let's see how powerful you think you are.

Score of 8 to 18. Powerful.

You think you are the boss. You believe that your effort or good luck makes things go well and that your errors or bad luck leads to problems. You do not believe that the world is ruled by other people. You may have some difficulty accepting direction from superiors. Keep in mind that no matter how much you want to be the ruler of your own kingdom, sometimes you have to do as you are told.

Extra low scorers: If you scored 8 to 10, remember, you are not Napoleon or Caesar. You may be better off being self-employed. If you are not, sometimes you have to do what you are told. You may as well grin and bear it.

Score of 19 to 28. Empowered.

Your score is in the mid-range. You believe that many things are within your control, yet recognise that you are not always in charge. You have a balanced perspective of when to defer to someone in authority and when you can be your own boss. You are probably a great employee.

Score of 29 to 40. Powerless.

You feel powerless. You believe that much of your life is governed by others. If you are young or still living with your parents, this may be your reality. If you are older and live independently, you must realise that your opinions count. You may expect others to dominate you too readily. Try to assert yourself when possible.

Extra high scorers: If your score is 37 to 40, people take advantage of you – and you let them. Go back and check your answers to the power questions and see if you have answered them truthfully. Start to give yourself some power. Begin by being a little more assertive with people you know well. Practise leading conversations and asking for what you want. Assign yourself more power in your daily interactions. Take this test again in six months to measure how far you have come.

How Do You Compare?

Now that you know *your* locus of control score – whether you are an internal or an external – think about how you compare to others who have taken part in locus of control studies. These experiments are organised into some of the major elements in life such as leisure, work and health.

HOW DO YOU SPEND YOUR LEISURE TIME?

As you might imagine, internals enjoy taking part in activities that require greater skill, and they prefer to play games that allow greater personal control, like chess, tennis and animated computer games. When given a choice of working on tasks that required either luck or skill, externals preferred tasks requiring luck; internals chose skill. Internals are more motivated to achieve success and they will play more competitively and cooperatively to win a game, whereas externals show a stronger belief in chance.

DO YOU LIKE ACTION TELEVISION?

British television analyst Dr Mallory Wober watches what you watch. He has studied the viewing diets of thousands of Americans and Brits and discovered that externals watch more action-adventure TV. This is important to broadcasters because he also found that TV stations can count on action programmes for reliable, big audiences. It seems that externals (along with teenagers and 'timid' people) can't get enough of the stuff. They are considered 'heavy users' – those who keep consuming programmes and never tire of the content.

WHAT DO YOU DAYDREAM ABOUT?

Even the simple act of daydreaming has not escaped psychological study. Three researchers from New York investigated how locus of control influences daydreams. They assessed the locus of control of two hundred college students and then measured the frequency and content of their daydreams. Their theory was confirmed: locus of control even affects our quiet musing. Internals tend to daydream about achieving things while externals contemplate fear of failure. The results make sense – internals believe they are capable of changing their lives and ponder self-empowering thoughts, while externals believe they are subject to the whims of chance and consider fearful consequences.

HOW ASTUTE IS YOUR SENSE OF HUMOUR?

Psychologists are not well known for their sense of humour, but they do study it from time to time. A Canadian journal describes a study where unsuspecting students are given a list of words to study. The students thought they were being tested on their verbal skills. However, embedded in an otherwise boring list of words were a number of words with a sexual double entendre (rubber, bust, screw). Internals were the first to realise they were being tricked and the first to smile and laugh about the situation. Externals took longer to realise they were being duped and were less ready to see the humour in this experimenter's practical joke. Why the difference? It seems that internals are sensitive to changes around them and pay greater attention to their body's signals, like the feeling of embarrassment.

A young graduate student conducted his own study and found similar results when he played a trick on his peers. Volunteers were told that they were being shown photographs of criminals. They leafed through a stack of disreputable-looking characters and took the task seriously, that is, until they came across their own photograph. Again, internals responded to the trick with a laugh and accepted being duped. However, the externals were less able to make light of an uneasy situation. Externals who are the butt of practical jokes are often irked rather than amused.

ARE YOU POLITICALLY ACTIVE?

Although the available research is mixed, some psychologists indicate that internals are more likely to participate in political action, such as joining demonstrations and signing petitions. One of the first studies asked African–American college students in the South to devote some of their vacation time to participate in the civil rights movement. Students were asked to volunteer for activities ranging from signing a petition to joining a march on Washington, D.C. Internals, who try to exert control at every level of their lives, were more interested in participating and wanted to make a difference.

ARE YOU OVERWEIGHT?

Locus of control theories once suggested that overweight people tended to be external. The argument stated that because internals accept greater responsibility for their actions, they would be extra careful about their diet and therefore thinner. However, this has never been proven. Externals come in all sizes. It could be that we are all susceptible to outside cues (like advertising) when it comes to eating. This suggests that even the most internal person can succumb to the sight and smell of food – even if the internal's body says that it is not hungry.

DO YOU PUT SALT ON YOUR FOOD?

You do? Say you are served a plate of chips. Internals strive for that last ounce of control over their lives, so they shake salt on their food *before* they taste it in a triumphant gesture that declares, 'I control my life!' Externals, on the other hand, accept what comes along in life, and they react to their circumstances. They taste their food first and then add salt.

DO YOU KNOW WHEN YOU'RE DRUNK?

A couple of psychologists tricked their student volunteers into thinking they were drinking rum and cola. They made up a placebo drink using a non-alcoholic rum extract, vanilla extract and cola. They then gave it to the students, and watched what happened. A fake Breathalyser was used to convince the volunteers they were legally drunk. The students then 'drove' in a driving simulator. What happened? The externals 'crashed' their cars! It seems that the externals looked for outside cues rather than their body's physical condition to tell them they were drunk. The externals were told they were drunk, so they acted drunk. The internals, on the other hand, apparently looked for cues within their bodies. They were not drunk; therefore, they did not make significantly more errors.

DO YOU ABUSE DRUGS?

Pamela Carlisle-Frank reviewed more than sixty drug and locus of control studies to determine what links personality to drug use. She found that contrary to what you might expect, chronic drug abusers, heroin addicts and alcoholics tend to have internal personalities. Although internals maintain greater control over most aspects of their lives, drug use must be considered separately. There is evidence that internals still believe that they have their drug and alcohol habits in control even when the external situation clearly suggests otherwise.

ARE YOU IN GOOD HEALTH?

Internals tend to be more fit and exercise more regularly than externals. They take better care of their teeth. When internals become ill, they seek out more information and confront health conditions. Because of this, internals are more knowledgeable about their maladies. This health-seeking behaviour is useful to those trying to prevent sickness. For example, when the Department of Health releases reports on diseases, it is the internals who study them and change their ways. Internals are far more likely to quit smoking when they are given information about cancers and lung disease. However, those who do smoke tend to be firm believers in the 'chance' aspect of locus of control.

DO YOU USE YOUR SEAT BELT?

Externals take whatever life throws at them. They do not seek control, and therefore they are less likely to buckle up their seat belts when in the car. And so it gets worse – externals are also more likely to be involved in car accidents.

DO YOU NEED THERAPY?

If you are currently seeing a therapist or have the opportunity to see one in the future, you may want to keep your locus of control score in mind. There is evidence to suggest that if you are an external, you would do better with a therapist who stresses his/her role as the director of your mental health. You may respond better if you put

your mental health in the hands of your therapist and plan on minimal input. If you are an internal, you would do better to take
responsibility for your own treatment. Get a therapist who encour-
ages you to develop your own goals and reinforcements (rewards
for meeting your goals). Be sure you can share your experiences
with your therapist.

ARE YOU JUST PLAIN ACCIDENT PRONE?

Several studies found that most accidents and injuries happen to
externals. A study of almost three hundred hospital employees found
that externals had significantly more accidents. Another project of
more than one hundred hotel workers found those who had major
accidents or who were sacked for unsafe behaviour were mostly
externals. The same holds true for many other occupations, including
bus drivers, football players and chemical plant employees!

ARE YOU ATTRACTIVE?

Dr Rosemarie Anderson, a social psychologist from Wake Forest
University, looked at physical attractiveness. She asked students to
come into her lab and complete a locus of control test. Her subjects
arrived one at a time, took the test and left. Unbeknownst to them,
they completed the quiz in front of a one-way mirror, behind which
sat a panel of judges who rated the attractiveness of each student.
Dr Anderson found that moderately attractive people are more
internal, but the very attractive and very unattractive tended to be

external. She suggests that the gorgeous and the ugly are stereotyped by the people they meet. Regardless of what they say and do, people treat them the same way. Both groups may believe that life is under external control because their behaviour does not influence others.

DO YOU USE CONTRACEPTION?

Did you know that your locus of control beliefs can affect your decision to use birth control? Two large studies, which interviewed hundreds of sexually active women in the United States and Australia, found that internals were much more likely to practise some form of birth control. Both studies, however, found that less than half of all sexually active women practised any contraception. We learned earlier that, on average, women tend to be more external than men. So when asked why they rebuff birth control, it was no surprise the non-practising women often said they 'leave such things to fate or luck'.

A separate Australian project also investigated the influence of locus of control on contraceptive practice, to a somewhat different result. Researchers interviewed pregnant women and found that, although internals had more favourable attitudes towards contraception, they were not more likely to *use* it. This is a clear example of how a personality trait can be measured, be seen to affect an attitude, but not be strong enough to change behaviour.

Of course, beliefs that make up locus of control can change. Perhaps experiencing an unplanned pregnancy reveals a lack of control and causes the mother to become more external. Even women who plan their pregnancies often talk about their babies 'taking over their bodies' as if they are hosts to an alien life-form. That can lead to developing an external personality.

HAS YOUR MAN HAD A VASECTOMY?

Drs Carment and Paluval demonstrated just how powerful locus of control can be in a study they published in the *Journal of Cross-Cultural Psychology*. They found that among men in India, locus of control was related not to whether they had a vasectomy but to the *reason* for having a vasectomy. Internals reported that the operation was a 'personal decision', mid-level men said it was a 'joint decision with wife', and surprise, surprise, externals reported that the 'wife made the decision'.

ARE YOU PERSUADED BY ADVERTISING?

If you are an external, you may be more persuaded by commercial messages. Internals realise that they are the subjects of persuasion and resist advertisers' attempts. In fact, some internals deliberately change their attitudes to the opposite of the advertisers' messages. To influence internals, you must present information that concerns them personally.

DO YOU CHEAT ON YOUR TAXES?

A couple of Dutch researchers found that internals were more likely to cheat on their taxes. They also discovered that internals were more likely to be business owners and, hence, had greater familiarity with tax laws. Although externals were less likely to cheat on their taxes, they were more likely to steal money.

HOW DO YOU BEHAVE AT WORK?

Among factory workers, internals set harder goals than externals. This is because internals believe that they can control their work by their own behaviour. But internals only work harder if they think that their hard work will lead to desirable outcomes, like pay increases, bonuses, promotions and recognition.

Internals do not look to others for direction. They would rather do things on their own, and they resist the control that supervisors impose. If you are an internal and you are dissatisfied at work, you are more likely to complain or quit. Internals will also try to control their work lives by setting their own work flow, changing procedures and modifying work assignments.

Because externals tend to be compliant, they look to others (like their supervisors) for guidance. Generally, externals are easier to supervise and follow directions well. Externals are in many ways better employees. However, the nature of the job has some bearing on how internals and externals operate. A job that requires independence, initiative, frequent changes in tasks and a great amount of information processing is best left to the internal. Externals are better suited to jobs that are routine in nature, such as production line, clerical and unskilled labour jobs.

ARE YOU A GOOD SUPERVISOR?

Several university studies found that internals are more likely to become leaders, internal leaders performed better than external leaders and the groups headed by internals performed significantly better than external-led groups. Internals have the advantage because they are goal oriented and focus on results. If given a chance to supervise, internals who find themselves in a position of power try to lead their employees through persuasion. Externals, on the other hand, select punishment to influence their employees.

To become a better supervisor (and employee), you must take your own, your supervisor's and your employees' loci of control into account. You need not test your co-workers, merely listen to how they attribute their triumphs and failures. To succeed as a supervisor, keep this important personality concept in mind: use the supervisory style that best suits the individual – direct for externals and participatory for internals.

CAN YOU CHANGE YOUR LOCUS OF CONTROL?

Locus of control is a tricky concept because it affects behaviour and, in turn, the consequences of that behaviour influence locus of control. Dr Krolick from Syracuse University discovered that internals shift towards externality after experiencing failure, but externals did not become internal after they experienced success. This may be because externals are less sensitive to situations that affect them, while internals are more sensitive to the results of their actions.

A study of small business owners whose businesses were damaged in a storm showed that changes can occur. The entrepreneurs took the locus of control test twice, once at eight months after the storm and then again at forty-two months after the disaster. Psychologists found that internals who were able to make their business profitable again shifted towards greater internality, and externals whose business deteriorated became more external. A similar study found that middle-aged men who had lost their jobs shifted toward externality.

If you are an external who would rather become more internal, the easiest thing to do is simply age! Evidence suggests that as individuals get older (from late teens to middle age), they become more internal. This is hardly surprising, given that most people actually do achieve greater control over their lives, obtaining greater personal and financial independence with advancing years.

7

PERSONALITY OVERVIEW

There's only one corner of the universe you can be certain of improving, and that's your own self. ALDOUS HUXLEY

We are tested and compared throughout our lives. When you were one minute old, a nurse gave you the first of thousands of tests that measure you throughout life. Your nurse wriggled your tiny legs, looked into your big baby eyes and even tickled your little baby feet to test your reflexes. She probably also gave you the first smile you ever saw. The nurse awarded you a score that compared you to millions of other infants. Your score was discussed with medical staff and your mother, and the comparisons started.

And just think of all the other tests we take! School tests in the years before our GCSEs, driving tests to get our first set of wheels, pregnancy tests, eye tests, vocational tests and physicals. There are tests to get into college, tests on our blood – and tests on our DNA, the very nature of our bodies, are now commonplace. And I can't tell you how many times I've told my children they are testing me!

It is not as though we don't enjoy making comparisons. In fact, it seems that as a species we are fanatical about judging others. We almost have an innate need to know how we compare to other people. We are obsessed with checking ourselves against models, celebrities and peers to see if our clothes are good enough, if our hair is full enough, if our loved ones love us enough. We examine how others treat their children. We gossip, chitchat and tittle-tattle. Even after we're dead, our obituaries are read so people can compare their lives to ours. We are tested from cradle to grave, and the comparisons still continue after we are gone.

The tests in this book, however, are voluntary. You can take them at your leisure, compare yourself to others in private, and consider whether you like your score just the way it is or if you'd like to work on a trait and improve it. The bottom line is that the final comparison is yours. I have a friend who says, 'The hardest part of going running is lacing up your shoes.' Congratulations on lacing up yours. Now let's see where you want to go.

A CONSTRUCTIVE OVERVIEW OF YOU

The tests and comparisons selected for this book were designed to take you on a guided tour of your personality. We focused on three main areas of your character:

1. **Your Hardware/Brain Power:** We started our tour at the top by measuring your brain power. We learned a little about how you are wired. Attributes like intelligence and creativity are tied closely to physiology. By measuring them, we explored just how powerful a machine your brain is.

2. **Your Social Skills:** Once you learned your cognitive strengths, we determined how well you apply them. Brains alone are not enough: you must successfully interact with fellow humans to be whole. After all, there are many brilliant people with dreadful social skills. We looked at core human needs: how well you relate to others and how skilful you are as a lover.

3. **Your Enthusiasm for Life:** The tour of your personality now reaches its peak. After learning what you *can* do, we measured what you are doing with your potential. These are the big questions in life. What brings you happiness? Do you take the credit for the work you do? Do you use your abilities to help others? Are you the boss of your life?

Now that you have taken the tests, learned something new about yourself and others, and maybe even had some fun, it is time to take a step back from your personality and view the larger picture. We are going to use the information we learned, and then you will be asked to consider yourself as a whole and compare what you are with what you would like to be.

After getting their test results, some people grow despondent because they have not measured up to their own standards. Nobody gets a top score on every test, and sometimes there is no 'top score'. Fortunately, most test takers decide which areas of their personalities they want to improve and work towards that improvement. The important thing to realise is that nobody is perfect. We all have strengths and weaknesses. We must accept the things we cannot change and work to improve the ones we can.

I want you to use this book to help yourself be you own best friend. Your best friend tells you the truth even if you may not want to hear it, because he or she cares for you. You can choose to use that information to help yourself – or not. Completing these tests is like that. With any luck, you have found parts of this book entertaining and perhaps informative. What you do with the information is up to you. Let's see how you scored compared to your wishes . . .

Your Personality Overview

To view your personality objectively, we will first review each area of your personality as measured, then evaluate yourself as a whole.

First, let's rate your qualities. Jot down your scores on the score sheet provided. If you skipped a test, just leave that section blank. Then do some soul-searching. You must ask yourself a hard question and give yourself an honest answer: how satisfied am I with my score? Perhaps it was lower than you wanted when you first took the test, but now, after considering other aspects of your personality, your score doesn't seem so bad. Is your IQ score as important as your Happiness score? Is your Creativity score more meaningful than your Locus of Control? It is entirely up to you to decide.

With the benefit of some distance between taking the test and reconsidering its outcome, and some reflection regarding which parts of your life are truly important, rank how satisfied you are with your scores on the tests you have taken.

Measuring Your Personality Overview

Using the table below, where '1' means not satisfied and '5' means satisfied, circle the number that best represents how satisfied you are with this particular aspect of your life.

HOW SATISFIED ARE YOU WITH YOUR PERSONALITY?

Test	Score	Not Satisfied			Satisfied	
Intelligence Quotient (IQ Test)	_____	1	2	3	4	5
Wordsmith's Creativity Test	_____	1	2	3	4	5
Engineer's Creativity Test	_____	1	2	3	4	5
Relationship Satisfaction Test	_____	1	2	3	4	5
Relationship Strength Test	_____	1	2	3	4	5
Sexual Opinions Test						
Permissiveness	_____	1	2	3	4	5
Responsibility	_____	1	2	3	4	5
Emotion	_____	1	2	3	4	5
Selfishness	_____	1	2	3	4	5
Sexual Experiences and Desires Test	_____	1	2	3	4	5

Happiness Test

Cheerfulness	_____	1	2	3	4	5
Seriousness	_____	1	2	3	4	5
Bad Mood	_____	1	2	3	4	5

Cheerfulness Test – Your Friend's Opinion

Cheerfulness	_____	1	2	3	4	5
Seriousness	_____	1	2	3	4	5
Bad Mood	_____	1	2	3	4	5

Peak Experiences Test	_____	1	2	3	4	5

Locus of Control Test

Internal/External	_____	1	2	3	4	5
Chance	_____	1	2	3	4	5
Power	_____	1	2	3	4	5

ANALYSING YOUR PERSONALITY: ARE YOU HAPPY WITH YOU?

Hardly anyone is perfectly satisfied with all elements of their life. Part of being human is the struggle for improvement. You must now focus your energy on improving those areas where you are least satisfied. One of the wonderful things about the personality traits we have studied is that they are malleable – they can be moulded into shape and improved. Our genes only determine a range within which each aspect of our personality must function. Of course, some parts of our personality are easy to change, whereas others, like raising your IQ, are particularly difficult.

IMPROVING YOUR IQ

There is a forest of books out there offering advice for those who wish to add a few points to their IQ score. However, most efforts to increase IQ are based on two outcomes: becoming a better test taker and retaining your mental acuity. Improving your test-taking ability is of limited use, but keeping your mental muscle fit is well worth the effort. Within physical boundaries, you can keep your mind sharp by stretching it daily. Reading, completing crossword puzzles, playing games, engaging in stimulating conversation and learning new things are all examples of enjoyable daily activities that keep your brain sharp.

For those of you hung up on IQ numbers, please remember the people who were clamouring to measure skulls and toes. Keeping your mind sharp is a wonderful thing, but devoting time to raising your IQ score a couple of points is not.

IMPROVING YOUR CREATIVITY

In chapter 2, we talked about the three main aspects of creativity we can measure:

Flexibility – the number of different types of ideas you can generate.

Fluency – the number of similar ideas you can generate.

Originality – the number of novel ideas you can generate.

While creative geniuses seem to be physiologically gifted, with their brains wired differently than others', there are plenty of useful exercises the rest of us can use to get that creativity muscle in shape. Many suggestions for improvement involve going out of your way to experience new stimuli. Some recommendations, like imagining you have a doorway that leads to anywhere in time or space, are wonderfully expansive without being expensive. If you would like to work specifically on improving or maintaining your creativity, review the suggestions in chapter 2. In addition, there are many books available that deal solely with creativity. Keep in mind that improving your creativity will help you improve other areas of life.

IMPROVING YOUR RELATIONSHIPS

Forming and maintaining solid relationships is vital to our species. In many ways, we are selfish beasts who pursue our own interests indiscriminate of those around us. But if it were not for our need to bond with one another, we would have become extinct millions of years ago. In fact, of all the elements of personality presented in this book, our ability to form satisfactory relationships may be the most important. Think about it: it does not matter whether you are a genius, creative or the hardest working person in the world if you can't effectively communicate your ideas to another. But there is a catch: while we need to form relationships, we don't all have the skills to make them satisfying or long lasting. Even the most charismatic among us find that building strong relationships takes hard work.

In addition to being the most important personality skill in this book, the ability to form relationships is also uniquely independent from the other traits mentioned. You can be in a wonderful relationship even if you did poorly on the other tests. People on their deathbeds want to be surrounded by their loved ones, not inventions and art.

The fact that relationship skills are free of other personality constraints can make an ordinary life extraordinary. You do not have to be brilliant and wealthy to be a good husband, wife, son or daughter. In the end, time spent with friends and loved ones tends to outweigh even the most successful career. Remember the old adage, 'Nobody ever died wishing they had spent more time at the office.' If you are not satisfied with your scores on the relationship tests, re-read the suggestions in chapter 3 and focus on improving this vital part of life.

IMPROVING YOUR SEXUAL ATTITUDES

A healthy sex life is important in our relationship satisfaction and our overall happiness in life. We have evolved to enjoy sex. It helps keep us in families and it is part of our heritage. But as you saw from the figures presented in 'Sex and Desire' there are plenty of myths and misunderstandings when it comes to the art of making love. Many of the problems with sexual relationships stem from societal pressures conflicting with our innate desire to mate. There is a grand battle being waged between our genes trying to express themselves and our desire to conform to social norms. This combat has kept clinical psychologists in fancy cars since fancy cars were invented.

The sexual attitudes test was selected for a reason: it has four fascinating subscales. You learned about your attitudes towards permissiveness, your tolerance of others, your opinions on the spiritual aspects of sex and whether you are a sexual game player. Also, I hope, you had the chance to share this test with your sexual partner. This test should have shown the nature of your sexual opinions and stimulated discussion with your partner. If you want to improve your attitudes toward sex, start with the four subscales and your partner's opinions. When it comes to sex, there is always a little room for improvement.

IMPROVING YOUR HAPPINESS

Happiness is like a thermostat that tells you if your life is functioning well. To enjoy a good life, you must be satisfied in many areas ranging from basic biological needs, like food and shelter, to the most psychological needs, like affection and emotional support.

With any luck, chapter 5 led you to think about important concepts in your life. While being smart, creative and a good lover are certainly positive attributes, being happy with yourself and your life is more important. Regardless of the score you got after taking the happiness tests, stop and contemplate your results. Are you getting what you need out of life? Do you enjoy your job? Does your life have purpose? If you got a score that is lower than you want, take heed of the suggestions for improvement. Also, bear in mind that our brains are wired individually. Some brains readily accept pleasant incidents and remember them, while others tend to focus on negative events and dwell on those. Knowing the ideas in the happiness chapter will help you improve your perspective, but, ultimately, you are in charge.

In some ways, your happiness score is a summation of your other scores. Chances are that if you are satisfied with most parts of life, your happiness score will be high. However, problems in one or two areas in your life will bring your happiness down. Therefore, it is important to address the root cause of unhappiness rather than cover it with a bandage. After all, if your thermostat says it is too cold, you don't take apart the thermostat and try to fix it. You heat up the room.

Apply the information you learned from the other tests about yourself to make your life happier. Perhaps you have found that you scored fairly low on a personality trait that you need for your job. Unless you can significantly improve in that area, your job may continue to make you miserable. If this sounds like you, you have three options: work at improving the skill necessary to do the job, change jobs for one that better uses your strengths, or reassess just how happy you want to be. If you do not want to change careers, you will need to turn down the happiness thermostat a little.

IMPROVING YOUR LOCUS OF CONTROL

Who is in control of your life? Do you accept whatever comes along in life, or do you take the bull by the horns and wrestle it to the ground? We have assigned values when discussing the other traits featured in this book. Most of us agree that we would rather be happy than unhappy, original rather than unoriginal and clever rather than foolish. But locus of control is a continuum with no 'good' or 'bad' ends.

Chapter 6, 'Motivation and Control', was designed to teach you about this psychological concept. If you believe it is better to be an internal or an external, you can work to accept greater or lesser control of your life. The important thing about locus of control is to know that it is there and how it affects you. To 'improve' your locus of control, you must pay attention to the motivations for your actions. Do not try to control things over which you have no power; you can't change the weather, so accept it. On the other hand, if your spending habits are the issue, take control of the situation by setting and following your own guidelines.

I particularly like the locus of control test because it measures three related but distinct concepts: control, chance and power. If your score indicated that you are an internal with a low belief in chance and high sense of power, you are a reliable self-starter who takes the bull by the horns and wrestles it to the ground daily. But if we tweak just one score and think about externals who don't believe in luck and feel they are powerful, a new personality appears: someone like an individual whose family has provided many comforts. Perhaps it's found in someone who has inherited wealth or someone who feels destined for greatness. Consider the combination of your three scores on this test; they may say something about your past and, if left unchanged, will guide your future.

IMPROVING YOURSELF

*People often say that this or that person has not yet
found himself. But the self is not something one finds;
it is something one creates.* THOMAS SZASZ

Unlike the ads on television promising instant improvement, your
personality is not some putty you can reshape in five short minutes.
You are a wonderful combination of your genes and your experiences.
It has taken years of effort to form you into the person you
are today. Changing that is not easy, but it can be done. You have
already completed the four important steps:

1. Learning about some elements of personalities.
2. Measuring yourself.
3. Learning how you compare to others.
4. Deciding what you would like to improve.

You may have found out that you are not all that different from
your neighbours. If you have worked through this book with a
friend, you should have been able to put yourself in that person's
shoes for a while. I hope that you have learned that you are a pretty
good person after all. But to be human is to seek improvement.
After all, we did not stop inventing after the first wheel was made.

If you have selected some areas of your life to work on, you have taken the fourth step towards self-improvement. Now, step five: *Get out there and do it*. Start with the smaller, easy-to-accomplish suggestions. Read books that deal with the trait you are seeking to improve, then apply the principles you have learned. Improve yourself incrementally. Use that personality muscle over and over, and retest yourself in a year. Work at becoming the person you want to be.

Being bright, creative and sexually enlightened are valuable traits, but being part of society is our destiny. We all enjoy the security of living among others in a community, but group membership has costs. Our independent, 'survival of the fittest' nature must compromise with our need for companionship. In order to live in groups and prosper, we sometimes have to behave in altruistic ways we would rather not. This is what good citizenship is all about.

The group of personality traits we have discussed culminates with good citizenship because in many ways, all the previous aspects of our behaviour combine in citizenship. If you picture your personality traits connecting like the processes of driving a car, your cognitive skills are the car, your social skills are the petrol, your motivation is the driver and your good citizenship tells you which is the right road to take. You have to do something with your skills or risk being an outcast. Improving your citizenship skills should start with small, easy steps to make life a little better for someone else, but like most important accomplishments, meaningful improvement comes with years of hard work.

Finally, your good health is key to all of the aspects of life we have discussed. Eating well, sleeping well and loving well are all key ingredients to a healthy personality. You will never be happy if you are always tired, and you will not be able to think as clearly with a belly full of chemicals and saturated fats. You do not have to be an athlete or fitness guru, but you do have to make the best of the body you have. Furthermore, your emotional needs must be met. Build bridges to your family and friends. Love others and, most of all, love yourself.

COMPARING OURSELVES TO ICONS

Nobody wants to be called common people,
especially common people. WILL ROGERS

The thoughts of famous characters appear throughout this book to illustrate certain concepts. The behaviour of these icons makes the personality trait being discussed more concrete. For example, it may be easier to understand internal locus of control given the image of Edison stooped over his lab desk, testing a thousand pieces of bamboo in an attempt to produce electric light. Many of us spend too much time comparing ourselves to actors and athletes. We can admire our icons, but we must be careful of trying to emulate them.

Being an icon is hard. Past idols we still admire were quite human. They faced the same temptations, had the same troubles and made many of the same mistakes as you and I. Although she was a tribute to sexuality, Marilyn Monroe was also a victim of sexual abuse. Pablo Picasso, like Albert Einstein, had an extremely difficult time forming relationships with women and children. Cleopatra, known for two thousand years for her ability to form lucrative relationships, killed her baby brother. And Martin Luther King, who did so much for all of us, had his personal life paraded throughout the media to his detractors' delight. So, while most of us can only marvel at Einstein's insights and King's commitment, we can also take comfort in realising that wildly special talents in one area often mean shortfalls in others.

Finally, you should know that comparing yourself to others is not an end in itself, but merely a tool to benchmark your abilities. Knowing your strengths and weaknesses brings insight as you work towards change. The tests in this book help you determine who you are. Only you know who you want to be. Therefore, the final comparison is yours.

EPILOGUE

I have a few other book ideas floating around, and I would like your help. If you have some wishes or suggestions for the next book, or if you have a favourite scholarly test or research paper you'd like to see included, please drop me a note at the address below or visit the website and send me an email. I cannot personally respond to each letter, but I will read them all with interest.

Andrew Williams
P.O. Box 1
Slater, IA 50244
USA

www.thetruthaboutyou.org

REFERENCES

CHAPTER 1: INTELLIGENCE

Baggette, W., and Tobacyk, J. J. Mensa membership and narcissism. *Psychological Reports,* 1988, 62(2), 434.

Beigel, H. G. Body height and mate selection. *Journal of Social Psychology,* 1954, 39, 257–268.

Darwin, C. The origin of species by means of natural selection. London: John Murray, 1859.

DeMartino, M. F. Sex and the intelligent woman. New York: Springer, 1974.

Frearson, W., Barrett, P., and Eysenck, H. J. Intelligence, reaction time and the effects of smoking. *Personality and Individual Differences,* 1988, 9(3), 497–517.

Heilbrun, A., Jr. Psychopathy and violent crime. *Journal of Consulting and Clinical Psychology,* 1979, 47, 509–516.

James, W. H. The norm for perceived husband superiority: A cause of human assortive marriage. *Social Biology,* 1989, 36(3-4), 271–278.

Jin, H. Q., Araki, S., Wu, K. X., Zhang, Y. W., and Yokoyama, K. Psychological performance of accident-prone automobile drivers in China: A case control study. *International Journal of Epidemiology,* 1991, 20(1), 230–233.

Kleinke, C. L., and Staneski, R. A. First impressions of female bust size. *Journal of Social Psychology,* 1980, 110, 123.

Lapsley, D. K., and Enright, R. D. The effect of social desirability, intelligence, and milieu on an American validation of the conservatism scale. *Journal of Social Psychology,* 1979, 107, 9–14.

Lombroso, C. Histoire des progrès de l'Anthropologie de la Sociologie Criminelles pendant les années 1895–1896. Trav. 4th Cong. Int. d'Anthrop. Crim. Geneva, 1896, 187–199.

Luntz Research. Cited in *Washington Post,* October 8, 1995, C5.

Mascie-Taylor, C. G. N. Spouse similarity for IQ and personality and convergence. *Behavior Genetics,* 1989, 19(2), 223–227.

Mascie-Taylor, C. G. N., Harrison, G. A., Hiorns, R. W., and Gibson, J. B. Husband-wife similarities in different components of the WAIS IQ test. *Journal of Biosocial Science,* 1987, 19(2), 149–155.

Mascie-Taylor, C. G. N., and Vandenberg, S. G. Assortative mating for IQ and personality due to propinquity and personal preference. *Behavior Genetics,* 1988, 18(3), 339–345.

Matarazzo, J. D. Wechsler's the measurement and appraisal of adult intelligence. 5th edition. Williams and Wilkins: Baltimore, 1972.

Matte, T. D., et al. Influences on variation in birth weight within normal range and within sibships on IQ at 7 years. *British Medical Journal,* 2001, 323, 310–314.

Rabbitt, P., and McInnis, L. Do clever old people have earlier and richer first memories? *Psychology and Aging,* 1988, 3(4), 338–341.

Retherford, R. D., and Sewell, W. H. How intelligence affects fertility. *Intelligence,* 1989, 13(2), 169–185.

Rosner, M., and Belkin, M. *Archives of Opthalmology,* as reported by *Associated Press,* November 1987.

Sandler, A. D., Watson, T. E., and Levine, M. D. A study of the cognitive aspects of sexual decision making in adolescent females. *Developmental and Behavioral Pediatrics,* 1992, 13(3), 202–207.

Smith, J. W., Schmeling, G., and Knowles, P. L. A marijuana smoking-cessation clinical trial utilizing THC-free marijuana, aversion therapy, and self-management counseling. *Journal of Substance Abuse Treatment,* 1988, 5(2), 89–98.

Walsh, A. Cognitive functioning and delinquency: Property versus violent offenses. *International Journal of Offender Therapy and Comparative Criminology,* 1987, 31(3), 285–289.

Wentzel, K. R. Does being good make the grade? Social behavior and academic competence in middle school. *Journal of Educational Psychology,* 1993, 85(2), 357–364.

Wilkinson, L., Scholey, A., and Wesnes, K. Chewing gum selectively improves aspects of memory in healthy volunteers. *Appetite,* 2002, 38, 235–236.

Wilson, D., Hammer, L. D., Duncan P. M., Dornbusch, S. M., Ritter, P. L.,

Hintz, R. L., Gross, R. T., and Rosenfeld, R. G. Growth and intellectual development. *Pediatrics*, 1986, 78, 646–650.

CHAPTER 2: CREATIVITY

Amabile, T. Cited in The art of creativity. *Psychology Today*, 1992, March/April, 41–46.

Barnett, L. A., and Kleiber, D. A. Concomitants of playfulness in early childhood: Cognitive abilities and gender. *Journal of Genetic Psychology*, 1982, 1414(1), 115–127.

Csikszentmihalyi, M. Creativity: Flow and the psychology of discovery and invention. New York: HarperCollins, 1996.

Feingold, A., and Mazzeila, R. Psychometric intelligence and verbal humor ability. *Personality and Individual Differences*, 1991, 12, 427–435.

Gondola, J. C., and Tuckman, B. W. Effects of a systematic program of exercise on selected measures of creativity. *Perceptual and Motor Skills*, 1985, 60, 53–54.

Humke, C., and Schaeffer, C. E. Sense of humor and creativity. *Perceptual and Motor Skills*, 1996, 82, 5443–5446.

Isen, A. M., Daubman, K. A., and Nowicki, G. P. Positive affect facilitates creative problem solving. *Journal of Personality and Social Psychology*, 1987, 52, 1112–1131.

Krug, R., Finn, M., Pietrowsky, R., Fehm, H., and Born, J. Jealousy, general creativity and coping with social frustration during the menstrual cycle. *Archives of Sexual Behavior*, 1996, 25(2), 181–199.

Lapp, W. M., Collins, R. L., and Izzo, C. V. On the enhancement of creativity by alcohol: Pharmacology or expectation? *American Journal of Psychology,* 1994, 107(2), 173–206.

Lawshe, C. H., and Harris, D. H. Purdue creativity test. West Lafayette, Ind.: Purdue Research Foundation, 1957.

Lowe, G. Group differences in alcohol-creativity interactions. *Psychological Reports,* 1994, 75, 1635–1638.

MacLeod, G. A. Does creativity lead to happiness and more enjoyment in life? *Journal of Creative Behavior,* 1973, 7(4), 227–230.

Mahon, N. E., Yarcheski, T. J., and Yarcheski, A. Loneliness and creativity in adolescents. *Psychological Reports,* 1996, 79, 51–56.

Mednick, S. A., and Mednick, M. T. Examiner's manual: Remote associates test form 1. Boston: Houghton Mifflin, 1967.

Schredl, M. Dream length and creativity: An opposite finding. *Perceptual and Motor Skills,* 1994, 78, 1297–1298.

Sitton, S. The messy desk effect: How tidiness affects the perception of others. *The Journal of Psychology,* 1984, 117, 263–267.

Wicker, F. W., Thorelli, I. M., Baron W. L., III, and Ponder, M. R. Relationships among affective and cognitive factors in humor. *Journal of Research in Personality,* 1981, 15, 359–370.

CHAPTER 3: RELATIONSHIPS

Ackerman, A. Natural history of love. New York: Random House, 1994.

Babbin, S. Kissing and its relationship to marital satisfaction. Ph.D. Dissertation Institute for Advanced Study of Human Sexuality, 1984.

Baron, R. A. Olfaction and human social behavior: Effects of a pleasant scent on attraction and social perception. *Personality and Social Psychology Bulletin*, 1981, 7(4), 611–616.

Blood, D. J., and Ferriss, S. J. Effects of background music on anxiety, satisfaction with communication, and productivity. *Psychological Reports*, 1993, 72, 171–177.

Borda, J. What do you want from me anyway? *Psychology Today*, June 1994.

Burns, J. A., and Kintz, B. L. Eye contact while lying during an interview. *Bulletin of the Psychonomic Society*, 1976, 7(1), 47–51.

Buunk, B. P., Angleiter, A., Oubaid, V., and Buss, D. M. Sex differences in jealousy in evolutionary and cultural perspective. *Psychological Science*, 1996, 7(6), 359–363.

DePaulo, B. M., and Kashly, D. A. Everyday lies in close and casual relationships. *Journal of Personality and Social Psychology*, 1998, 74(1), 63–79.

Dutton, D. G., and Aron, A. P. Some evidence for heightened sexual attraction under conditions of high anxiety. *Journal of Personality and Social Psychology*, 1974, 30, 505–518.

Felmlee, D. H. Be careful what you wish for: A quantitative and qualitative investigation of fatal attractions. *Personal Relationships*, 1998, 5, 235–253.

Goldberg, T. L. Altruism towards panhandlers: Who gives? *Human Nature*, 1995, 6(1), 79–89.

Grewen, K. M., Anderson, B. J., Girdler, S. S., and Light, K. C. Warm partner contact is related to lower cardiovascular reactivity. *Behavioral Medicine*, 2004.

Hecht, M., Larkey, L., and Marston, P. The love ways inventory. *Journal of Social and Personal Relationships*, 1994, 11, 25–44.

Mattel. Barbie sales figures from Mattel web page, September 1998.

Morin, R. The golden years. *Washington Post,* April 7, 1996.

Morin, R. Love, marriage, and race. *Washington Post,* September 9, 1995.

Muscarella, F., and Cunningham, M. R. The evolutionary significance and social perception of male pattern baldness and facial hair. *Ethology and Sociobiology,* 1996, 17, 90–117.

Norton, K. I., Olds, T. S., Olive, S., and Dank, S. Ken and Barbie at life size. *Sex Roles,* 1996, 34(3-4), 287–294.

Pennebaker, J. W., Dyer, M. A., Caulkins, S., Litowitz, D. L., Ackreman, P. L., Anderson, D. B., and McGraw, K. M. Don't the girls get prettier at closing time: A country and western application to psychology. *Personality and Social Psychology Bulletin,* 1979, 5, 122–125.

Sigelman, L., Dawson, E., Nitz, M., and Whicker, M. L. Hair loss and electability: The bald truth. *Journal of Nonverbal Behavior,* 14, 1990, 269–283.

USA Today snapshot. How often people lie. January 1, 1998.

Wiseman, R. The truth test survey. Cited in the *Montgomery Express* (Va.), June 8, 1994, A9.

Zajonc, R. B., Adelmann, P. K., Murphy, S. T., and Niedenthal, P. M. Convergence in physical appearance of spouses. *Motivation and Emotion,* 1987, 11(4), 335–347.

CHAPTER 4: SEX AND DESIRE

Ackerman, D. A natural history of love. New York: Random House, 1994.

Allgeier, E. R., and Fogel, A. F. Coital positions and sex roles: Responses to cross-sex behavior in bed. *Journal of Consulting and Clinical Psychology,* 1978, 46, 588–589.

Baker, R. Sperm wars: The science of sex. New York: Basic Books, 1996.

Barrash, D. P., and Lipton, J. E. Making sense of sex: How genes and gender influence our relationships. Washington, D.C.: Island Press, 1997.

Cutler, W. B., and Preti, G. Hormones and behavior, 1987, 20, 463–482.

Cutler, W. B., Preti, G., Krieger, A., Huggins, G. R., Garcia, C. R., and Lawley, R. J. Human axillary secretions influence women's menstrual cycles: The role of donor extract from men. *Hormones and Behavior*, 1986, 20, 474–482.

Eberhard, W. G. Sexual selection and animal genitalia. Cambridge, Mass.: Harvard University Press, 1984.

Hendrick, S., and Hendrick, C. Multidimensionality of sexual attitudes. *Journal of Sex Research,* 1987, 23, 502–526.

LoPiccolo, J., and Steger, J. The sexual interaction inventory: A new instrument for assessment of sexual dysfunction. *Archives of Sexual Behavior* 1974, 3, 585–595.

Manning, J. T. Fertility pointers. Cited in *Des Moines Register.* September 21, 1998, T1.

McKinney, K., and Sprecher, S., eds. Sexuality in close relationships. Hillsdale, N.J.: Lawrence Erlbaum Associates, 1991.

Michael, R. T., Gagnon, J. H., Laumann, E. O., and Kolata, G. Sex in America: A definitive survey. Boston: Little, Brown, 1994.

Money, J. The destroying angel. Buffalo, N.Y.: Prometheus Books, 1985.

O'Sullivan, L. E. Less is more: The effects of sexual experience on judgments of men's and women's personality characteristics and relationship desirability. *Sex Roles,* 1995, 33(3-4), 159–181.

Robinsion, J., and Godbey, G. Who has most sex? *American Demographics,* February 1998.

Rossi, A. S., ed. Sexuality across the life course. Chicago: University of Chicago Press, 1994.

Scheib, Joanna. *Evolution and Human Behavior,* 1997, 18, 143–149.

Scheib, J. E., Kristiansen, A., and Wara, A. A Norwegian note on 'Sperm donor selection and the psychology of female mate choice.' *Evolution and Human Behavior,* 1997, 18(2), 143–150.

Simmons, G. L. Sex and superstition. London: Harper & Row, 1973.

Student, J. No sex, please, we're college graduates. *American Demographics,* February 1998.

Vital STATS. No sex please, we're educated. *Newsletter of the Statistical Assessment Service,* February 1998, 1.

Wilson, W., and Liedtke, V. Movie-inspired sexual practices. *Psychological Reports,* 1984, 54, 328.

CHAPTER 5: HAPPINESS

Anderson, C. A., Deuser, W. E., and DeNeve, K. M. Hot temperatures, hostile affect, hostile cognition, and arousal: Tests of the general model of affective aggression. *Personality and Social Psychology Bulletin,* 1995, 21(5), 434–448.

Bryden, M. P., Free, T., Gagné, S., and Groff, P. Handedness effects in the detection of dichotically-presented words and emotions. *Cortex,* 1991, 27(2), 229–235.

Campbell, S., and Murphy, P. Extraocular circadian phototransduction in humans. *Science,* January 16, 1998.

Christenfeld, N., Phillips, D. P., and Glynn, L. M. What's in a name? Mortality and the power of symbols. Paper presented at the 19th Annual Meeting of the Society of Behavioral Medicine, New Orleans, La., March 1998.

Crocker, J., and Gallo, L. The self-enhancing effect of downward comparison. Paper presented at the American Psychological Association Convention, Los Angeles, August 1985.

Diener, E., and Diener, C. Most people are happy. *Psychological Science,* 1996, 7, 181–185.

Dillon, K. M., Minchoff, B., and Baker, K. H. Positive emotional states and enhancement of the immune system. *International Journal of Psychiatry in Medicine,* 1985, 15(1), 13–18.

Ehrlichman, H., and Halpern, J. N. Affect and memory: Effects of pleasant and unpleasant odors on retrieval of happy and unhappy memories. *Journal of Personality and Social Psychology,* 1988, 55(5), 769–779.

El Nasser, H. Age-old question: Why so healthy? *USA Today.* December 29, 1997.

Forgas, J. P., and Bower, G. H. Mood effects on person-perception judgments. *Journal of Personality and Social Psychology,* 1987, 53(1), 53–60.

Gurin, G., Veroff, J., and Feld, S. Americans view their mental health: A nationwide interview survey. New York: Basic Books, 1960.

Harrison, D. W., Gorelczenko, P. M., and Cook, J. Sex differences in the functional asymmetry for facial affect perception. *International Journal of Neuroscience,* 1990, 52, 11–16.

Inglehart, R. Culture shift in advanced industrial society. Princeton N.J.: Princeton University Press, 1990.

Isen, A. M., and Levin, P. F. Effects of feeling good on helping: Cookies and kindness. *Journal of Personality and Social Psychology,* 1972, 21, 384–388.

Milberg, S., and Clark, M. S. Moods and compliance. *British Journal of Social Psychology,* 1988, 27, 79–90.

Orbuch, T. L., House, J. S., Mero, R. P., and Webster, P.S. Marital quality of the life course. *Social Psychology Quarterly,* 1996, 59(2), 162–171.

Philpot, V. D., and Madonna, S. Fluctuations on mood state and learning and retrieval. *Psychological Reports,* 1993, 73, 203–208.

Ruch, W., Kohler, G., and van Thriel, C. Assessing the 'humorous temperament': Construction of the facet and standard trait forms of the State-Trait-Cheerfulness-Inventory (STCI). *Humor: International Journal of Humor Research,* 1996, 9, 303–339.

Salovey, P., and Birnbaum, D. Influence of mood on health-relevant cognitions. *Journal of Personality and Social Psychology,* 1989, 57(3), 539–551.

Sato, T. Seasonal affective disorder and phototherapy: A critical review. *Professional Psychology: Research and Practice,* 1997, 28(2), 164–169.

Twenge, J. M., and Campbell, W. K. *Journal of Marriage and Family,* 2003, 66.

Unconvential wisdom. *Washington Post,* June 4, 1995, C5.

Veenhoven, R. Happy life-expectancy: A comprehensive measure of quality-of-life in nations. *Social Indicators Research,* 1996, 39, 1–58.

What the wealthy would pay for? *USA Today,* snapshot, December 1997.

CHAPTER 6: MOTIVATION AND CONTROL

Adame, D. D., Johnson, T. C., Cole, S. P., Matthiasson, H., and Abbas, M. A. Physical fitness in relation to amount of physical exercise, body image, and locus of control among college men and women. *Perceptual and Motor Skills,* 1990, 70, 1347–1350.

Anderson, C. Locus of control, coping behaviors, and performance in a stress setting: A longitudinal study. *Journal of Applied Psychology,* 1977, 62, 446–451.

Anderson, C. R., and Schneier, C. E. Locus of control, leader behavior and leader performance among management students. *Academy of Management Journal,* 1978, 21, 690–698.

Anderson, R. Physical attractiveness and locus of control. *Journal of Social Psychology,* 1978, 105, 213–216.

Blignault, I., and Brown, L. B. Locus of control and contraceptive knowledge, attitudes and practice. *British Journal of Medical Psychology,* 1979, 52, 339–345.

Brannigan, G. G., Hauk, P. A., and Guay, J. A. Locus of control and daydreaming. *The Journal of Genetic Psychology,* 1990, 152(1), 29–33.

Breckenridge, R. L., and Dodd, M. O. Locus of control and alcohol placebo effects on performance in a driving simulator. *Perceptual and Motor Skills,* 1991, 72, 751–756.

Bridge, R. G. Internal-external control and seat-belt use. Paper presented at the meeting of the Western Psychological Association, San Francisco, 1971.

Caldwell, J. C., Young, C., Ware, H., Lavis, D., and Davis, A. Australia: Knowledge, attitudes and practice of family planning in Melbourne. *Studies in Family Planning,* 1971, 4, 49–59.

Carlisle-Frank, P. Examining personal control beliefs as a mediating variable in the health damaging behavior of substance use: An alternative approach. *Journal of Psychology,* 1991, 125(4), 381–397.

Carment, D. W., and Paluval, T. R. Correlates of birth control practices in India. *Journal of Cross-Cultural Psychology,* 1973, 4, 111–119.

Foon, A. E. Locus of control as a predictor of outcome of psychotherapy. *British Journal of Medical Psychology,* 1987, 60(2), 99–107.

Garza, R. T., and Ames, R. E. A comparison of Anglo- and Mexican-American college students on locus of control. *Journal of Consulting and Clinical Psychology,* 1974, 42, 919.

Goodstadt, B. E., and Hjelle, L. A. Power to the powerless: Locus of control and the use of power. *Journal of Personality and Social Psychology,* 1973, 27, 190–196.

Gore, P. M., and Rotter, J. B. A personality correlate of social action. *Journal of Personality,* 1963, 31, 58–64.

Groenland, E. A., and Van Veldhoven, G. M. Tax evasion behavior: A psychological framework. *Journal of Economic Psychology,* 1983, 3(2), 129–144.

Hansen, C. P. Personality characteristics of the accident-involved employee. *Journal of Business and Psychology,* 1988, 2(4), 346–365.

Hoyt, M. F. Internal-external control and beliefs about automobile travel. *Journal of Research in Personality,* 1973, 288–293.

Kabanoff, B., and O'Brien, G. E. Work and leisure: A task-attributes analysis. *Journal of Applied Psychology,* 1980, 65, 596–609.

Kahle, L. R. Stimulus condition self-selection by males in the interaction of locus of control and skill-chance situations. *Journal of Personality and Social Psychology,* 1980, 38, 50–56.

Krolick, G. Changes in expectancy and attribution following success, failure, and neutral consequences. Doctorial dissertation, Syracuse University, 1978.

Leeton, J. The incidence of unwanted pregancy in Australia. *The Medical Journal of Australia,* 1975, l, 821–824.

Lefcourt, H. M. Reseach with the locus of control construct: Volume 3, extensions and limitations. Orlando, Fla.: Academic Press, 1984.

Lefcourt, H. M., Gronnerud, P., and McDonald, P. Cognitive activity and hypothesis formation during a double entendre word association test as a function of locus of control and field dependence. *Canadian Journal of Behavioral Science,* 1973, 5, 161–173.

Lester, D. Cooperative/competitive strategies and locus of control. *Psychological Reports,* 1992, 71(2), 594.

Levenson, H. Activism and powerful others: Distinctions with the concept of internal-external control. *Journal of Personality Assessment,* 1974, 38, 377–383.

Lundy, J. R. Some personality correlates of contraceptive use among unmarried female college students. *Journal of Psychology,* 1972, 80, 9–14.

MacDonald, A. P. Internal-external locus of control and the practice of birth control. *Psychological Reports,* 1970, 27, 206.

Morrison, D. M. Adolescent contraceptive behavior: A review. *Psychological Bulletin,* 1985, 98(3), 538–568.

Parnes, H. S., and King, R. Middle-aged job losers. *Industrial Gerontology,* 1977, 4, 77–95.

Smith, H. L., and Dechter, A. No shift in locus of control among women during the 1970s. *Journal of Personality and Social Psychology,* 1991, 60, 638–640.

Sordoni, C. Experiments in humor: Creativity, locus of control and their relationship to two dimensions of humor. Unpublished doctoral dissertation, University of Waterloo, 1979.

Spector, P. E. Behavior in organizations as a function of employee's locus of control. *Psychological Bulletin,* 1982, May, 91(3), 482–497.

Williams, A. F. Personality characteristics associated with preventative dental health practices. *Journal of the American College of Dentists,* 1972a, 30, 225–234.

Williams, A. F. Factors associated with seat belt use in families. *Journal of Safety Research,* 1972b, 39(4), 133–138.

Wober, M. The extent to which viewers watch violence-containing programs. Special issue: Violence on television. *Current Psychology Research and Reviews,* 1988, 7(1), 43–57.

Yukl, G. A., and Latham, G. P. Interrelationships among employee participation, individual differences, goal difficulty, goal acceptance, goal instrumentality, and performance. *Personnel Psychology,* 1978, 31, 305–323.

INDEX

acceptance 119, 176, 214-15
accident proneness, and internal/external personalities 254
addiction to love 104-5
adolescence 83-4
advertising 125, 156, 256
affection, and relationship success 119
African Americans, locus of control beliefs 234
age, preferences for partners 33
alcohol, effects on creativity 73-4
alcoholism, and internal/external personalities 252
Allgeier, Elizabeth 158
Amabile, Teresa 74
American women, locus of control beliefs 234-5
Ames, R.E. 234
Anderson, Rosemarie 254-5
anger 219-19, 223
apes, comparisons with humans 2-3
Aron, Arthur 105-6
attraction, when it turns to repulsion 116
attractiveness
  and internal/external personalities 254-5
  and perfume 113-14
  and relationship success 118
  and stereotyping 254-5
  changing assessment of 107
  effects of exercise 109-10
  perceptions of baldness 108-9
  perceptions of beards 108
autonomy, and happiness 176

Babbin, Sylvia 117
babies, interaction with parents 82-3
Bad Mood score see Cheerfulness Test
baldness, perceptions of 108-9
Barbie, chances of meeting a live one 114
beards, perceptions of 108

beauty, and happiness 176
beliefs see also Locus of Control Test
  about effects of personal effort 229, 230-1
  about luck 229, 230-1
  about personal control 234-5
  about success 229, 230-1
  and social and economic status 234-5
bell curve distribution of test scores 25
Berscheid, Ellen 86
Binet, Alfred 4-5
birth weight, and IQ 28
blood pressure 218
Blood, Deborah 106-7
boys, effects of birth weight on IQ 28
brain
  attempts to increase IQ 37-8
  effects of insulin 38
  endorphins released by kissing 118
  keeping your mind sharp 268

brain power, aspect of
  personality 263
brain size, used to measure
  intelligence 3, 4
breasts, size and perception of
  intelligence 34
Brown, James 127
Bryden, Philip 219

Campbell, Scot 225
car accidents, and
  internal/external
  personalities 253
Carlisle-Frank, Pamela 252
Carment, D.W. 256
chance, belief in see Locus of
  Control Test
Cheerfulness Test 178 see
  also Happiness Test; Peak
  Experiences Test
  Bad Mood score 201-2
  Cheerfulness score 197-9
  instructions 185
  questions 186-90
  scoring 196-7
  Seriousness score 199-200
Cheerfulness Test for Your
  Friend (about you) 178
  Bad Mood score 201-2
  Cheerfulness score 197-9
  instructions 190-1
  questions 191-5
  scoring 196-7
  Seriousness score 199-200
children
  encouraging creativity in
    74-5
  indications of IQ 28-9
  learning relationship skills 83
  relationships with friends 83
  style of humour 73
citizenship skills, combination
  of personality traits 276
city living, and sexual
  permissiveness 157
Clark, Margaret 221
Cleopatra 278
committed love 104
communication, importance
  in relationships 119, 166-71

companionate love 103
compatibility, and
  relationship success 119
competition, as creativity
  killer 75
conformity, and happiness
  176
Congreve, William 106
contraception use 31, 255-6
control see locus of control
convergence, between
  partners 32
Coolidge, Calvin 5
couples, deciding when to
  start having sex 155
craniometry, used to measure
  intelligence 3-4
creation myths 42
creative personality
  acquiring knowledge 44-5
  and gender roles 68
  and loneliness 70-1
  and risk taking 70
  breaking the rules 68-9
  complexity of 67-75
  dreaming and inspiration
    45-6
  emotional oscillations 69
  finding an audience 46-7
  implementing ideas 46
  ingredients of 43-7
  introversion and
    extroversion 68
  loving to work 46
  paradoxes of 68-9
  questioning and analysing 45
  standing alone 44
  taking risks 43-4
  telling jokes 70
creativity 42-3
  causing happiness 73
  dreaming 72
  effects of alcohol 73-4
  effects of ovulation 77
  effects of rewards on 71
  encouraging in children 74-5
  flexibility 53-4
  fluency 54
  improved by running 71-2
  in primitive cultures 42

  link to wit and humour 73
  originality 54
  persistence 71
  solving life's problems 73
  use of symbols 42-3
  using mind mapping 75-7
  ways to improve 75-9, 269
creativity killers 74-5
creativity testing
  history of 47-8
  Purdue Engineer's Creativity
    Test 47-8, 53-67
  Wordsmith's Creativity Test
    48-53
criminal behaviour
  methods used to predict 3, 4
  types related to IQ 34-5
Crocker, Jennifer 225
crying 217, 218
Csikszentmihalyi, Mihaly
  69-70
cultural bias in intelligence
  tests 5

danger, and falling in love
  105-6
Darwin, Charles 2
daydreams, and
  internal/external
  personalities 249
delinquency, and IQ 34-5
DeMartino, Manfred
dependability, and good
  relationships 121
depression
  actions you can take 183-4
  and feelings of helplessness
    242-3
  seasonal affective disorder
    (SAD) 224-5
  summer 225
  winter 224-5
Diener, Carol 211
Diener, Ed 178, 211
Dillon, Kathleen 217
divorce, stage when couples
  consider it 216
dreaming, and creativity 72
driving safety, link with IQ
  29-30

drug abuse, and internal/external personalities 252
drunkenness awareness, and internal/external personalities 252
Dutton, Donald 105-6

Edison, Thomas 231-2, 277
education
 and sexual activity 160
 and sexual permissiveness 157
 mean IQ scores for levels of 29
Ehrlichman, Howard 219-20
Einstein, Albert 1, 278
emotional needs, and healthy personality 277
employees, and internal/external personalities 257
endorphins, released by kissing 118
Engineer's Creativity Test (Purdue) 47-8
 instructions 53-5
 questions 56-63
 scoring 64
 what your score means 65-7
Enright, Robert 32
enthusiasm, and relationship success 119
enthusiasm for life, aspect of personality 263
ethnic bias in intelligence tests 5
ethnicity, variations in age of first intercourse 154
European Americans, locus of control beliefs 234
evolution, and intelligence measurement 2-3
excitation transfer 109-10, 223
exercise, and attraction 109-10
expectations, and good relationships 121
'external' personalities 232

see also Locus of Control Test
accident proneness 254
alcoholism 252
and action television programmes 248-9
and contraception use 255-6
and drug abuse 252
and political activism 250-1
and weight 251
as employees 257
as supervisors 258
attitude to healthy living 253
awareness of being drunk 252
best style of therapy for 253-4
car accident risk 253
daydreams 249
effects of advertising on 256
leisure pursuits 248
level of attractiveness 254-5
reason for having a vasectomy 256
salting food 251
seat belt wearing 253
sense of humour 250
shifts in locus of control 258-9
smoking 253
social and economic status 234-5
stealing money 257
tax cheating 256-7
work behaviour 257
extroversion, in creative personalities 68
eye contact, and lying 115

faces, detecting emotion in 218-19
fame, and happiness 176
fatal attraction, attraction changes to repulsion 116
fatalism see 'external' personalities
father, women's criteria for choosing 158-9
Felmlee, Diane 116
Ferriss, Stephen 106-7

fingers, used as measure of fertility 156-7
flexibility, and creativity 53-4
fluency, and creativity 54
Fogel, Alan 158
forearms, used to measure intelligence 3, 4
forehead height, used to measure intelligence 3, 4
friends, importance of 83-4, 176

Gallo, Lisa 225
Garza, R.T. 234
genes
 and jealousy 110-12
 and personality 268
 effects on men's behaviour 110-12, 112-13
geniuses, testing for levels of 5
girls, effects of birth weight on IQ 28
glasses (wearing), link with IQ 34
goals, and happiness 176
Goldberg, Tony 112-13
Goldwyn, Sam 229
good deeds, and happiness 221-2
Goodman, Roy M. 173
graham crackers, as cure for masturbation 165
Graham, Sylvester 165
Grewen, Karen 118
growth, and happiness 177
gum chewing, to increase IQ 37-8

hair and baldness in men 108-9
Halpern, Jack 219-20
handholding, health benefits of 118
happiness 174-5
 acceptance and 176, 214-15
 as an outlook on life 177
 as internal monitor 174
 as subjective well-being 173
 autonomy and 176

beauty and 176
conformity and 176
detecting in faces 218-19
detecting in voices 219
doing good deeds and 221-2
effects of acts of kindness
  222
effects of laughter on
  immune system 217
effects of pleasant smells
  219-20
effects on health 217
effects on judgement 222-3
effects on learning and recall
  221
fame and 176
finding Mr Right 175
friends and 176
goals and 176
growth and 177
happiest stage of your life
  215-16
helping creativity 72-3
intelligence and 176
life expectancy and 214
light levels and 224-5
loving relationships and 176
money and 214-15
optimism and 176
perfectionism and 176
personal control and 176
positive outlook and 176
possessions and 176
power and 176
purpose in life and 176
realism and 176
self-esteem and 176
sexual permissiveness and
  157
special talent and 176
stagnation and 177
status and 176
types of unhappiness 174-5
ways to feel happier 225-7,
  272-3
wealth and 176
what people would pay for it
  215
what you don't need to be
  happy 175-7

what you need to be happy
  175-7
winning the lottery and 175
wisdom and 176
work you enjoy and 176
happiness filter, concept of
  181, 182-3
happiness ratings 211-12
Happiness Test 178 see also
  Cheerfulness Test; Peak
  Experiences Test
concept of 'happiness filter'
  181, 182-3
concept of 'pleasant effect'
  181
concept of 'unpleasant effect'
  181
instructions 179
questions 180
scoring 181
what your score means
  183-5
happiness testing, history of
  177-8
Happy Life Expectancy, for
  various countries 212-13
Harris, Doug 47, 63
headaches, as reason not to
  have sex 160
health
benefits of physical contact
  118-19
effects of happiness 217
effects of humour on 217
healthy living
  and internal/external
    personalities 253
importance for healthy
  personality 277
height
  and IQ 28
  preferences for partners 33
helplessness see 'external'
  personalities
Hendrick, Clyde 130
Hendrick, Susan 85-6, 130
Hispanic Americans, locus of
  control beliefs 234
honesty, and relationship
  success 119

hugging, health benefits of
  118
humans, comparisons with
  apes 2-3
humour
  and internal/external
    personalities 249-50
  and long life 214
  effects on health 217
  in children 73
  link to creativity 73
Huxley, Aldous 261

icons, dangers of trying to
  emulate 277-8
immune system 118, 217
infidelity 110-13
ingenuity, tapping into 75-7
initials, and life expectancy
  216
innate abilities, measurement
  of 6
inspiration, during restful
  interludes 46
insulin, effects on the brain
  38
intelligence 1-38 see also IQ
  (intelligence quotient);
  Mensa organisation
  and happiness 176
  and relationship success 119
  methods used to measure 2-5
  without knowledge 36
intelligence tests see IQ
  (intelligence quotient) Test;
  IQ tests
'internal' personalities 230-2
  see also Locus of Control
  Test
  accident risk 254
  alcoholism 252
  as employees 257
  as supervisors 258
  awareness of being drunk
    252
  best style of therapy for 253,
    254
  car accident risk 253
  contraception use 255-6
  daydreams 249

drug abuse 252
effects of advertising on 256
healthy living 253
leisure pursuits 248
level of attractiveness 254-5
political activism 250-1
reason for having a
  vasectomy 256
salting food 251
seat belt wearing 253
sense of humour 250
shifts in locus of control
  258-9
smoking 253
stealing money 257
tax cheating 256-7
weight 251
work behaviour 257
introversion, in creative
  personalities 68
intuitive love 103
inventive creativity see
  Purdue Engineer's Creativity
  Test
IQ (intelligence quotient)
  attempts to increase 37-8
  birth weight and 28
  bust size used to judge 34
  calculation of 2, 4
  childhood indications of 28-9
  choice of partner and 32-3
  clarity of early memories and
    37
  delinquency and 34-5
  effects of chewing gum 37
  effects of marijuana use 35-6
  effects of smoking 37
  height and 28
  link to number of children
    33-4
  link with being teacher's pet
    29
  link with contraceptive use
    31
  link with driving safety
    29-30
  link with good behaviour at
    school 29
  link with nearsightedness 34
  link with wearing glasses 34

nerd stereotype and 34
  preferences for partners 32-3
  racial prejudice and 32
  scores for various education
    levels 29
  sexual fantasies in women
    and 31
  types of criminal behaviour
    and 34-5
  ways to improve 268
IQ (intelligence quotient) Test
  (Mensa) 6
  comparison with other
    groups 27-36
  distribution of scores 25-7
  questions 7-21
  scoring 22-5
  scoring categories 25-7
  what your score means 25-7
IQ tests
  cultural bias of 5
  history of 2-5
  origins of 4-5
  race and ethnic bias 5
  standardisation of 4-5
  what they measure 1, 2
Isen, Alice 222

James, William 33
Japanese women, locus of
  control beliefs 234-5
jazz, and frequency of sex
  164
jealousy, gender differences in
  110-12
joke telling, and the creative
  personality 70
judgement, as creativity killer
  75

Ken, chance of meeting a live
  one 114
kindness, effects of acts of
  222
King, Martin Luther 278
kissing 117-18
Krolick, G. 258-9

language barriers in
  intelligence tests 5

Lapp, William 74
Lapsley, Daniel 32
Lawshe, Chuck 47, 63
learning, improved in happy
  people 221
Lefcourt, Herbert 234
leisure pursuits, and
  internal/external
  personalities 248
Levenson, Hanna 236
Levin, Paul 222
life expectancy
  and happiness 214
  and initials 216
  and marriage 119-20
  and overall happiness
    (various countries) 212-13
  how to live to 100 214
light levels, and happiness
  224-5
Lincoln, Abraham 225-6
listening, and good
  relationships 121
locus of control 229-31 see
  also 'external' personalities;
  'internal' personalities;
  Locus of Control Test
  and social and economic
    status 234-5
  changing 258-9
  history of testing 233-5
  influence on behaviour 230-1
  influence on motivation 231
  ways to improve 273-4
Locus of Control Test 235-6
  Belief in Chance score 240-1,
    244-6
  instructions 236
  Internal/External score
    240-1, 242-4
  Power score 240-1, 246-8
  questions 236-40
  scoring 240-1
Lombroso, Cesare 3
loneliness, and the creative
  personality 70-1
LoPiccolo, Joseph 147
love
  addiction to 104-5
  assessing attractiveness 107

commitment and 84-5
committed 104
companionate 103
dating someone of another
  race 109
effects of PEA
  (phenylethylamine) 104-6
holiday romances 105
in dangerous situations
  105-6
intimacy and 84
intuitive 103
marrying outside of your
  race 109
romantic 84
secure 104
traditional 104
type of 103-4
wartime romances 105
lovesickness 84, 104
Lowe, Geoff 73-4
luck, beliefs about 229, 230-1
lying 114-16

Manning, John 156-7
marijuana use, effects on
  intelligence 35-6
marriage
 and longer life 119-20
 growing to look like your
   spouse 120
 health benefits of 119-20
 stages of happiness 215-16
 strains caused by children
   215-16
Mascie-Taylor, Nick 32
masturbation, and graham
  crackers 165
Mathes, Eugene 179
Mednick, Martha 48, 50
Mednick, Sarnoff 48, 50
memory
 attempts to improve 37-8
 early memories and IQ 37
 improved in happy people
   221
 recall affected by odours
   219-20
men
 age of sexual peak 128

age preference for partner
  33
and beards 108
and crying 217, 218
benefits of being married
  119-20
causes of jealousy 110-12
creative personalities 68
creativity and humour 73
decision when couples start
  having sex 155
detecting anger in faces
  218-19
detecting happiness in faces
  218-19
effects of genes on behaviour
  110-12, 112-13
effects of oxytocin during
  sex 161
family size and IQ 33-4
hair and baldness 108-9
height preference for partner
  33
IQ preference for partner
  32-3
range of penis size and shape
  159
reasons for first having sex
  155
reasons for having a
  vasectomy 256
response to different
  approaches 164
variations in age of first
  intercourse 154
views on how women dress
  113-14
views on women's perfume
  113-14
working together with
  partner 168
Mensa IQ (inteligence
  quotient) Test 6
distribution of scores 25-7
questions 7-21
scoring 22-5
scoring categories 25-7
what your score means 25-7
Mensa organisation 6, 27
and narcissism 30

sexual fantasies of high IQ
  women 31
mental age testing 2, 4
messy desk, viewed as
  creative 69-70
Mexican Americans, locus of
  control beliefs 234
Milberg, Sandra 221
mind mapping, tapping into
  creativity 75-7
money 71, 214-15
monogamy 156
Monroe, Marilyn 125, 278
Montessori, Maria 4
motivation 231 see also locus
  of control
Murphy, Patricia 225
music 106-7, 164
musicians, attraction of 156-7

Nash, Ogden 174
nearsightedness, link with IQ
  34
nerd stereotype, and IQ 34
normal distribution of test
  scores 25

odours, effects on memory
  recall 219-20
office, messy and tidy desks
  69-70
old age, happiness in 84-5
optimism, and happiness 176
Orbuch, Terri 215-16
orgasm 161-2
The Origin of Species
  (Darwin) 2
originality, and creativity 54
overweight, and
  internal/external
  personalities 251
ovulation, effects on
  creativity 77
oxytocin 160-1

Paluval, T.R. 256
partner, choice affected by IQ
  32-3
PEA (phenylethylamine), and
  love addiction 104-5

peak experiences scale 179, 202-3
Peak Experiences Test 203-4
  see also Cheerfulness Test; Happiness Test
  instructions 203-4
  questions 205-8
  scoring 209
  what your score means 210-11
penis, range of sizes and shapes 159
perfectionism, and happiness 176
perfume, and attractiveness 113-14
persistence, and creativity 71
personal control 176, 234-5
  see also Locus of Control Test
personal effort, beliefs about effects of 229, 230-1
personal power, beliefs about see Locus of Control Test
personality
  genetic aspects of 268
  sexually active type 163
personality overview 261-78
  areas for improvement 267-8
  comparing yourself with your ideal 264
  comparisons with icons 277-8
  creation of good citizens 276
  deciding what you want to improve 264
  determining who you are 278
  getting your emotional needs met 277
  improving your creativity 269
  improving your happiness 272-3
  improving your IQ 268
  improving your locus of control 273-4
  improving your relationship skills 270-1

improving your sexual attitudes 271-2
measuring brain power 263
measuring enthusiasm for life 263
measuring social skills 263
need to compare our lives to others 261
Personality Satisfaction Measurement 265-7
steps towards improving yourself 275-6
taking care of your health 277
Personality Satisfaction Measurement 265-7
phenylethylamine (PEA), and love addiction 104-5
Picasso, Pablo 41, 43-4, 278
pleasant effect, concept of 181
political activism, and internal/external personalities 250-1
positive outlook, and happiness 176
possessions, and happiness 176
power
  and happiness 176
  beliefs about see Locus of Control Test
pressure, as creativity killer 75
prudishness 157
Purdue Engineer's Creativity Test 47-8
  instructions 53-5
  questions 56-63
  scoring 64
  what your score means 65-7
purpose in life, and happiness 176

race
  dating outside of your own 109
  marrying outside of your own 109

variations in age of first intercourse 154
racial bias in intelligence tests 5
racism, and IQ 32
reaction time, to measure intelligence 37
realism, and happiness 176
recall, improved in happy people 221
regrets 224
Relationship Closeness Inventory see Relationship Strength Test
Relationship Satisfaction Test 85-6
  instructions 86-7
  questions 87-8
  scoring 88-9
  what your score means 89-92, 100
relationship skills 82-5, 270-1
Relationship Strength Test 86, 92
  instructions 93
  questions 93-8
  scoring 99-100
  what your score means 100-2
relationship testing, history of 85-6
relationships 81-122
  and human capacity for sex 126-7
  deciding when to start having sex 155
  happiness and 176
  health benefits of 119-20
  importance of trust 114-15
  long-term 84-5
  need for 81-2
  requirements for success 118-19
  self-worth and 81
  ways to improve 102-3, 118-19, 121-2
  ways to improve your sex life 166-71
  what makes them last 118-19

religion, and sexual
  permissiveness 157
Remote Associates Test
  (RAT) 48, 50 *see also*
  Wordsmith's Creativity Test
Retherford, Robert 33-4
rewards, effects on creativity
  71
risk-taking, and creativity
  43-4
Rogers, Will 277
romance, and good
  relationships 122
Rotter, Julian 233-4, 235
Ruch, Willibald 178-9, 200
rules, as creativity killer 75
running, to improve creativity
  71-2

sadness
  and doing good deeds 221-2
  and regrets 224
  detecting in voices 219
  effects on judgement 222-3
salting food, and
  internal/external
  personalities 251
Satisfaction with Life Scale
  see Happiness Test
Scheib, Joanna 158
school
  being teacher's pet and IQ 29
  being the class clown 73
  good behaviour and IQ 29
scores, normal distribution
  (bell curve) 25
seasonal affective disorder
  (SAD) 224-5
seat belt wearing, and
  internal/external
  personalities 253
secure love 104
self-esteem 121, 176
self-improvement, steps
  towards 275-6
self-worth, and relationships
  81
sense of humour, and
  internal/external
  personalities 249-50

Seriousness score *see*
  Cheerfulness Test
sex
  age of first intercourse 154
  and partnerships 126-7
  as a marketable commodity
    125
  deciding when to start 155
  how long it lasts 129
  human capacity for 126-7
  in adolescence 83-4
  in advertising 125, 156
  monogamy 156
  number of partners 155-6
  privacy of 125-6
  prudishness 157
  public side of 125-6
  public's curiosity about 125-6
  putting off due to headaches
    160
  racial and ethnic variations
    154
  reasons for first starting 155
  romantic love and 84
  thinking about 125
  variety of methods and
    positions 129
  what stimulates people 129
  who we have it with 129
sex drive
  age of sexual peak 128
  and ageing 128-9
sex flush, before orgasm 163
sex life
  importance of
    communication 166-8
  length of 128
  role playing 170
  satisfaction in later life 128-9
  ways to improve 166-71
  ways to spice up 168-71
sexual activity level
  and education 160
  and love of jazz 164
  and money 162
  and personality traits 163
  frequency of 162-3
  who has the most sex 162-3
sexual assertiveness, in
  women 157-8

sexual attitudes
  desirable attributes 153
  improving 271-2
  undesirable traits 153-4
  virginity seen as appealing
    153
sexual behaviour testing,
  history of 130
sexual chemistry, effects of
  oxytocin 160-1
Sexual Experiences and
  Desires Test 147
  instructions 148
  questions 149-50
  scoring 151
  what your score means
    151-3
sexual fantasies, in high IQ
  women 31
sexual maturity 128
sexual myths 165-6
Sexual Opinions Test, 130-1
  Emotional score 145-6
  instructions 131
  Permissiveness score 140,
    141-3
  questions 132-7
  scoring 138-40
  Selfishness score 146-7
  Sexual Responsibility score
    143-4
sexual pairing, and human
  society 127
sexual permissiveness, factors
  associated with 157
Sitton, Sarah 69
skull size, used to measure
  intelligence 3-4, 4
smells, effects on memory
  recall 219-20
Smith, James 35-6
smoking 37, 253
social and economic status,
  and locus of control beliefs
    234-5
social learning theory 233-4
social skills, aspect of
  personality 263
society, based on sexual
  pairing 127

sperm donor, women's criteria
  for choosing 158-9
spouses
  'husband superiority'
    argument 33
  similarity in IQ 32-3
stagnation, and happiness
  177
standardisation of intelligence
  tests 4-5
status, and happiness 176
stealing money, and
  internal/external
  personalities 257
stereotyping, and
  attractiveness 254-5
stress, helped by hugs 118
subjective well-being see
  happiness
success in life, beliefs about
  229, 230-1
summer depression 225
supervisory skills, and
  internal/external
  personalities 258
surveillance, as creativity
  killer 74
symbols, use in creativity
  42-3
Szasz, Thomas 275

talent, and happiness 176
tallness in childhood and IQ
  28
tax cheating, and
  internal/external
  personalities 256-7
teacher's pet, link with IQ
  29
television viewing choice, and
  internal/external
  personalities 248-9
testing, throughout life 261-2
therapy, best style for
  internal/external
  personalities 253-4
toes, used to measure
  intelligence 3, 4
togetherness, and good
  relationships 121

traditional love 104
trust 114-15, 117

U.S. Army, use of intelligence
  tests 5
unhappiness, types of 174-5
unpleasant effect, concept of
  181

Van Gogh, Vincent 46-7
vasectomy, reason for having
  256
Veenhoven, Ruut 212
verbal skills testing see
  Wordsmith's Creativity Test
virginity 153, 154
voice, showing emotions in
  115, 119

wealth, and happiness 176
Wentzel, Kathryn 29
Wilson, Darrell 28
winter depression 224-5
wisdom, and happiness 176
Wober, Mallory 248-9
women
  age of sexual peak 128
  age preference for partner 33
  and crying 217, 218
  and seasonal affective
    disorder (SAD) 224
  benefits of being married
    119-20
  breast size and milk
    production 161
  bust size and perception of
    intelligence 34
  causes of jealousy 110-12
  creative personalities 68
  creativity and humour 73
  criteria for long-term mate
    158-9
  criteria for sperm donor
    158-9
  criticism of other women
    157-8
  deciding when couples start
    having sex 155
  detecting anger in faces
    218-19

detecting happiness in faces
    218-19
  effects of oxytocin on 160-1
  effects of style of dressing
    113-14
  effects of wearing perfume
    113-14
  family size and IQ 33-4
  height preference for partner
    33
  IQ preference for partner
    32-3
  locus of control beliefs
    234-5
  multiple orgasms 161
  ovulation and creativity 77
  perceptions of bald men
    108-9
  perceptions of beards on
    men 108
  reasons for first having sex
    155
  response to different
    approaches 164
  sex flush before orgasm 162
  sexual fantasies and high IQ
    31
  social penalties for sexual
    assertiveness 157-8
  variations in age of first
    intercourse 154
  working together with
    partner 168
Wordsmith's Creativity Test
    48-9
  instructions 49
  questions 50
  scoring 51
  what your score means 52-3
work behaviour, and
  internal/external
  personalities 257
work you enjoy, and
  happiness 176
worldliness, and sexual
  permissiveness 157

youth, and sexual
  permissiveness 157